£15.99

Whose Choice?

Contentious issues for those working with people with learning difficulties

Edited by
Judith Coupe O'Kane
and **Juliet Goldbart**

Foreword by
Professor Peter Mittler CBE

David Fulton Publishers
London

David Fulton Publishers Ltd
2 Barbon Close, London WC1N 3JX

First published in Great Britain by
David Fulton Publishers 1996

Note: The right of the contributors to be identified as the authors of their work has been asserted by them in accordance with the Copyright, Designs and Patents Act 1988.

British Library Cataloguing in Publication Data

A catalogue record for this book is available from the British Library

ISBN 1-85346-363-9 ✓

Typeset by Textype Typesetters, Cambridge
Printed in Great Britain by BPC Books and Journals Ltd, Exeter

Contents

Foreword

Judith Coupe O'Kane and Juliet Goldbart

'Sexuality', 'age-appropriateness' and 'integration' are three terms commonly used by those of us who are personally or professionally involved in the lives and development of children and adults with learning disability (in particular severe learning difficulties: SLD). We each feel we know what we mean by these terms, but do we? When we use them we assume that everyone knows what we mean by them, but do they? We tend to assume that all others understand them in the same way, but do they?

Our aim in editing *Whose Choice?* is to present a range of viewpoints which will stimulate discussion. The book is intended for a wide audience: our professional colleagues, the parents and carers of people with whom we work and, wherever possible, people with learning disabilities themselves. We hope that it will provoke ongoing debate, leading to clarification of what is understood, meant and expected by sexuality, age-appropriateness and integration.

In order to ensure this diversity of viewpoints in each of the three topics, we have invited colleagues from a range of backgrounds and professional stances to address selected issues according to their own perspectives. Sometimes these are complementary, sometimes contradictory, but in all cases they are informed by a balance between theory, professional practice and personal conviction. The third chapter on each topic involves a discussion of issues raised in the two preceeding chapters, expanding and enlarging on critical points.

Peter Mittler's Introduction establishes an overview of the concepts underpinning the book by promoting the notions of choice and advocacy for children and adults with special educational needs and their families – concepts that must be developed and nurtured.

Part 1 is entitled 'Sexuality for whom?' In Chapter 1, Maggie Bowen explores dilemmas raised by the impact of changing attitudes towards the status of people with SLD. Using case studies to illuminate key issues, she enables us to work through to practical, sensitive resolutions. Caroline Downs and Ann Craft, in Chapter 2, develop notions of sexuality with particular reference to people with profound and multiple disabilities. They describe the early stages of a valuable research project in this complex, little understood area. In Chapter 3, Ian McKinlay provides us with 'hard data' on puberty and sexuality in adolescents and young adults with SLD. He focuses particularly on the parents' perspective and provides a context for the previous two chapters.

Age-appropriateness is the focus of Part 2. Melanie Nind and Dave Hewett (Chapter 4) challenge the concept of age-appropriateness head on, contrasting it with developmental-appropriateness. The latter concept, they argue, has much to contribute to the development of social and communication skills in people with very severe disabilities. In Chapter 5, Jill Porter, Nicola Grove and Keith Park eloquently address age-appropriateness with particular reference to how schools can promote or prevent the development of age-appropriate behaviour. Beryl Smith, in Chapter 6, enhances our understanding of both age-and developmental-appropriateness, teasing out relationships and tensions between them.

Part 3 is 'Integration for whom?' For John Hall, integration is a matter of principle rather than academic debate. In Chapter 7, his analysis of models of 'segregated' education leads to his justification of the fundamental right of all children to attend their community school. Pat Conway and Paul Baker, in Chapter 8, critically examine evidence for the social and educational advantages of integration and the means by which token placements in mainstream schools can be avoided. They direct us to consider how both social participation and educational outcomes can be used to evaluate the quality of integrated education. In Chapter 9, Peter Farrell seeks a way forward. Taking into account the issues raised in the preceeding two chapters, he clearly identifies a range of viable alternatives for politicians and educationalists to consider when planning for an optimal quality of integrated education.

In addition to the specific topics at the centre of this book, certain key themes recur through the chapters, reminding us that the topics are linked by issues of both philosophy and practice. For Porter, Grove and Park, for example, changing society's willingness to accept people with learning disabilities is a valid, but long-term, objective. For Hall, and Nind and Hewett, however, it is a much more immediate imperative. Transition, too, is an overarching theme in many of the book's chapters. It is not very many years since people with SLD passed through childhood, adolescence and adulthood with few, if any, of the rites of passage most of us expect. Changing attitudes to childhood and to people with SLD are obliging us to address these transitions with sensitivity. Other themes, such as advocacy, normalization, autonomy and the need for forward planning permeate the book. Of crucial importance is the development and implementation of good practice. Indeed, all our authors would support the right of children and adults with learning difficulties to be major contributors to the decisions and choices affecting their own lives.

We, as editors, are excited and stimulated by these chapters. The scope of the book, *Whose Choice?*, we feel, promotes a deeper understanding of the issues we considered to be particularly important, yet controversial, in the lives of children and adults with such learning difficulties. Whilst we accept that many other issues remain important and contentious, we hope this book will contribute to the long-term debate and decisions made which affect and advance the lives of the very children and adults we wish to assist.

INTRODUCTION

Laying the Foundations for Self-advocacy: The Role of Home and School

Peter Mittler

Introduction

The right of people with learning disabilities to speak for themselves and to be listened to is increasingly accepted in many countries. But rights are not the same as reality. It is one thing to accept the principle of self-advocacy; making it happen is another.

We need to think about new ways in which the family can help to lay the foundations for self-determination on which their sons and daughters can build. At the same time, we must also recognize the difficulties faced by parents in doing this and the tensions which can arise for the family as a whole as young people gain the confidence to assert themselves and insist on their right to be heard. These are difficulties faced by all families but there may be additional problems when the young people have a significant learning disability.

The literature on self-advocacy is written largely from an adult perspective without reference to its origins in childhood. It says remarkably little about how families and schools can work together to lay the foundations for self-determination and personal autonomy. Indeed, where parents are mentioned, it is more in terms of emancipation from overprotection than as a source of support for self-advocacy.

Origins

The concept of self-advocacy does not have a simple or agreed definition. At its most basic individual level, it is concerned with the opportunity to make choices and decisions on day-to-day matters. During childhood, most of these opportunities will occur at home and at school. Later, more fundamental issues are involved, concerned with choice of job, where and how to live, leisure and recreation, choice of friends and partners, marriage and parenthood. Underlying this process is the growth of personal autonomy and ways in which this can be assisted or hindered by the family, the school and the whole range of personal and institutional influences which impinge on the person with a learning disability.

The self-advocacy movement has its origins in individuals getting together, initially in small groups to provide mutual support but increasingly finding the strength and the voice to articulate their views, needs and demands to a broader audience – for example to decision-makers who run the services in which they are involved. To this end, they may set up service user groups, perhaps with the aid of a support worker. Other self-advocacy groups make representations to service planners and providers in their area, to elected and appointed political representatives, as well as to the media and to the public as a whole.

But the capacity and confidence to speak for oneself does not appear overnight; it has to be fostered and encouraged over a period of years, long before effective participation in self-advocacy activities normally takes place. There is therefore a need for teachers and parents to work together to devise learning experiences which will help to lay the foundations. A recent book on empowerment of pupils with severe learning disabilities (Coupe-O'Kane and Smith, 1994) provides examples of innovative practices in schools but little information is available generally on how teachers and parents can work together to achieve these aims.

My concern in this chapter is primarily with the role of the family in relation to self-advocacy, but I would like to set this in context by providing a number of examples of areas of activity where the self-advocacy movement and individual self-advocates have been effective and influential. Although encouraging and inspirational, these examples suggest that self-advocacy for people with learning disabilities is still at an early stage of development and that much more could be achieved if conscious efforts were made by families and professionals in partnership to lay the foundations for advocacy skills, and if more opportunities can be created for self-advocates to express their views and to modify the views of others concerning their ability to become full citizens of their local and national communities, as well as citizens of the world.

International level

Disabled people have exerted a major influence on the United Nations. Until 1992, it was nearly always highly articulate disabled people with physical or sensory impairments who attended UN meetings and advocated powerfully on behalf of all disabled people. To do this, they needed to have physical access to the buildings, documentation in braille or tape and interpretation in sign language. But in October 1992, a special session of the United Nations General Assembly was held to mark the end of the Decade of Disabled Persons; on that occasion the General Assembly was addressed by Ms Barbara Goode, a Canadian self-advocate and elected member of the Executive Council of the International League. These are her words:

I speak on behalf of persons with mental handicap. We are people first - and only secondly do we have a handicap.

We want to push our rights forward and we want to let other people know we are here. We want to explain to our fellow human beings that we can live and work in our communities.

We want to show that we have rights and responsibilities.

Our voice may be a new one to many of you but you'd better get used to hearing it.

Many of us still have to learn how to speak up. Many of you have to learn how to listen and how to understand us.

We need people who have faith in us. You have to understand that we, like you, do not want to live in institutions. We want to live and work in our communities.

We count on your support to people with mental handicap and their families. We count on your support to ILSMH and its member associations.

Above all, we demand that you give us the right to make choices and decisions regarding our own lives.

There is a 'no applause' rule at all UN meetings. But the world's ministers spontaneously broke that rule in response to this speech.

Barbe Goode may be exceptional. But there are many more like her who have the ability and the commitment to participate in decisions affecting their lives and those of other people with learning disabilities. In order to be a member of the League's Council she needs a support person to help her go through the papers before the meeting, to interpret what is being said and sometimes to help her to say what she wants to say as effectively as possible. But her needs are not fundamentally different from non-disabled members of the Council who need support and assistance in coping with meetings which are held in a foreign language or the personal and technical supports needed by people with visual, hearing or physical impairments.

People with learning disabilities have planned and run their own international conferences, with support where this was agreed to be needed. The first international meeting of self-advocates was held in Washington State, USA in 1982; another was held in London in 1988 and the most recent conference in Toronto was attended by more than 1,300 self-advocates, including 200 from the UK.

Since 1982, the International League of Societies for Persons with Mental Handicap (now known as Inclusion International) has strongly encouraged self-advocates to contribute to its world congresses. Of course, mere presence – just 'being there' – cannot be equated with real participation. On the contrary, a congress can segregate and isolate people with learning disabilities by failing to take positive steps to ensure that as much of the conference as possible is accessible in every sense of the word. This includes physical access; ensuring that what is being said can be understood; being encouraged to make a real contribution as an equal; being listened to, rather than just being politely heard; avoiding tokenism or total acceptance of what is said merely because it is said by a person with a learning difficulty, rather than engaging in discussion.

It may sometimes be convenient for financial and other reasons for self-advocates to be accompanied by their parents. This can be useful if parents then keep in the background as much as possible and encourage their son or daughter to find their own friends and take part in the general activities of a conference. I have a painful memory of a father who stood immediately behind his daughter on the speaker's rostrum, guiding her finger across the page of a typed statement which she read out slowly and painfully but which she may well have been able to deliver without his assistance.

National level

At the national level, an increasing number of disabled people are on the boards of their national movements in fields such as visual, hearing or physical impairments. But how many people with learning disabilities are on the board of their national societies? What are the obstacles to their making a significant contribution to its discussions?

The relationship of the 'official' organizations to self-advocacy groups varies from country to country. In some countries, self-advocacy groups are a special interest group within the national organization, comparable to other special interest groups for parents of children with specific impairments (such as Down's Syndrome) or at points of transition (e.g., pre-school, school age, school leaving). They have considerable autonomy, set their own agenda and take part in annual meetings of the national society as a whole.

People with learning disabilities are, probably more than any other group, disadvantaged by the fact the others have always spoken for them. This includes the 'official' specialist voluntary organizations, composed mainly of parents but also professional groups who speak about the needs of people with learning disabilities on the basis of many years experience of working with them. There are therefore some major obstacles to their 'finding a voice', particularly if their own parents are prominent in national societies or local branches.

In some cases, such groups have felt that their views were not being heard or found themselves in disagreement with aspects of the policies or practices of the national society. For example, self-advocacy groups have successfully objected to the MENCAP logo, depicting a sad, helpless and pathetic child which had formed the foundation of fund-raising campaigns over 40 years. Suggestions were made that this image be dropped in favour of publicity depicting adults in more positive stances and in valued activities. In Canada, self-advocates were the deciding voice in changing the name of the society from Canadian Association for Mental Retardation to Canadian Association for Community Living.

Because of these ambiguities and tensions, people with learning disabilities have set up their own self-advocacy groups which are independent of the official voluntary organization, so that they could develop and pursue their own policies and campaigns, even when this involved opposition to the main 'parent' organization.

Obvious difficulties can arise where parents and their adult sons and daughters may attend the same meetings and conferences but find themselves in disagreement over one or more issues of policy. In the past, the young person may simply have accompanied the parents to meetings without any assumptions that they were understanding very much about the proceedings. But the time will come when this is no longer the case.

Disagreements between parents and their growing children on social and political issues are commonplace. But how often do families go out of their way to encourage their son or daughter with a learning disability to develop and express their own views, even if these differ fundamentally from those of their parents? Is it then possible to discuss differences openly within the family? Such discussions would provide valuable opportunities for young people to formulate and defend their views in discussions and debate within the family circle. The skills learned might then be put to good use outside the family.

All parents have to learn to accept that the views of their children are likely to differ from their own, sometimes on fundamental matters. But this process may be delayed or denied where young people with learning disabilities are concerned. Some parents may find it hard to accept that their son or daughter is able to think through the issues and come to an informed opinion of their own. They may simply assume that they either have no views on a particular subject or that they will automatically have the same opinions as their parents.

Obvious examples concern the issue of special or ordinary schools, independent living, supported employment or sexuality and sex education. But even more fundamental issues may be involved. I recall an occasion when parents (and some of their children) were attending a scientific session on developments in the area of primary prevention at an international conference. One young adult with Down's Syndrome turned to her companion and said, 'Did you hear? They want to stop people like us being born.'

Local level

At local level, self-advocacy groups may consist of individuals who come together from different services to discuss ways in which disabled people can gain access to local services and facilities. All disabilities tend to be represented, including people with learning disabilities. The groups are often known as 'coalitions' and many are federated in a national movement, such as the British Council of Organisations for Disabled Persons.

In other cases, users from a particular service form a 'users committee' to discuss specific issues arising from that service. Nearly ten years ago, a survey of day centres for adults with learning disabilities in the UK established that more than half of day centres had an established committee of this kind. This figure had doubled over the previous six years (Crawley, 1988). Other committees have been established in residential units, such as hospitals and hostels.

An increasing number of schools are setting up student committees, particularly for over-16s. Such committees help students to learn about working with others, including committee skills, such as addressing the chairperson, waiting for others to finish speaking, keeping to the point, listening and responding to others' point of view and perhaps modifying views in the light of discussion. Winup (1994) has provided a particularly interesting account of the establishment and development of such a committee.

Some community self-advocacy groups have become quite militant when they feel that the interests of disabled persons are being ignored or if they are not fully consulted on issues which concern them. This may be a cause of concern or conflict with the families, not only because of militant behaviour such as picketing a town hall or stopping traffic, but because parents may take the view that the authorities are already doing all they can.

Conflicts can also arise if parents and young people disagree on the appropriate service provision. This can be acute at the school-leaving stage. For example, parents may feel that the most appropriate placement is a day centre, while the young person may prefer a further education college. Similar issues may arise about the most appropriate form of residential service, for example, hostel, group home, supported independent living, etc.

The conventional approach to these problems is a joint case conference involving all parties, including the young person and the family. These are useful, but the power balance of such conferences is heavily weighted towards professionals. A recently explored alternative is that of service brokerage. This allows the individual concerned to consider various alternatives and to weigh the advantages and disadvantages of different forms of provision. The families have a major role to play, but one role of the service broker is to try to anticipate and resolve disagreements within a framework of discussion rather than confrontation. Resolution of conflicts and disagreements is not always possible; in the last analysis, the interests of the person with learning difficulties must be paramount.

The Role of Families

How, then, can families facilitate or frustrate the development of autonomy and independence in their sons and daughters?

A person with a learning disability may be a successful self-advocate as a service user, or at the national or international level. But the same individual may experience serious frustrations in their own family, just as the family may well feel that their son or daughter is 'not ready' for the independence on which they insist. These are problems for the family as a whole to discuss and resolve together, with support and help from others, if this is agreed to be necessary. It should not be seen as an inevitable conflict of interest and will.

Disagreements and conflicts about independence are part of the experience of every family and are generally resolved with time, though not without pain. But the situation of families where there is a relative with a learning disability may present additional challenges.

First, the son or daughter may be living with their family for many years (sometimes decades) after they would normally have left home. It is not uncommon for families to be responsible for their adult son or daughter into their 40s and 50s; indeed, some people with learning disabilities have in effect become full-time carers for their increasingly dependent parents. Ironically, they then join the armies of other unpaid and ignored carers in the community, usually women, who have given up the possibilities of leading their own lives, doing a job and developing personal and sexual relationships of their own, in order to meet the needs of one or more dependent relatives.

Disagreements about independence are therefore more prolonged in families where there is a relative with a learning disability. Such conflicts need not be overt or out in the open. The person with a learning disability may appear to acquiesce in the wishes of their parents but still feel bitterly resentful that there are many freedoms which are denied to them, for reasons which are no longer discussed and which may never have been adequately explained in the first place.

Second, it is common for the abilities and potential of people with learning disabilities to be seriously underestimated both by their families and by the professional staff with whom they come into contact. There is then a vicious circle in which parents believe that their child would not benefit from a particular activity or experience on account of their intellectual or physical limitations. Because they are deprived of the opportunity, they do not learn, thus appearing to confirm the original assumption. Examples include learning to swim, horse riding, camping, or joining a club. Other examples include cooking, making friends, going to shops or to social or sport events. Some parents oppose these activities on the grounds that their child is 'not ready' or that they pose too many dangers.

Some professionals alienate parents by insisting that their 'child' now has adult status and that the views of parents can if necessary be discounted. This attitude is misguided and unnecessarily confrontational, especially if the young person is living with the family. In assuming their main responsibility as carers, it is natural for parents to express concerns and anxieties. These need to be taken seriously.

Parents who have enjoyed successful partnership and dialogue with teachers while their child was at school may be bitterly disappointed when such collaboration does not continue after school leaving, on the grounds that it is somehow incompatible with the principles of normalization and age-appropriate behaviour. This is a simplistic view and, moreover, one that may actually undermine programmes which aim to foster autonomy and independence. It is unfortunate that too many professionals still ignore the family dimension or regard parents as inevitable obstacles to the independence of their son or daughter.

The natural wish of parents to protect their child's interests and to avoid failure experiences is understandable and should be respected. But many misunderstandings and breakdowns in communication could be avoided if parents, professionals and young people themselves are able to work together from the outset to plan in advance for ways in which they can jointly and severally collaborate to further the growing independence and autonomy of the individual concerned.

This process begins at an early age and includes using every available opportunity to provide choices – choice between two types of food or drink or articles of clothing; whether to have a story now or later and many other ordinary examples of everyday choices and decisions.

Mary Lodge and her son Christopher (1994) have written an illuminating account of how the family was determined from the earliest days of Christopher's life to ensure that he had every possible opportunity for exercising choice and decision-making, with the ultimate goal of self-advocacy and personal autonomy in mind from the beginning. Ironically, little is said about their history of collaboration with teachers, mirroring the lack of references to parents in teachers' accounts of their work in preparing for self-advocacy.

Every opportunity should be provided to enable even very young children to exercise some degree of control over their environment. Children should be given experiences which enable them to understand that it is their actions that determine what happens, whether it is turning a switch, opening a tap, splashing water or operating a computer. Even from an early age, they will come to appreciate the ways in which language and communication can be used to influence the environment and other people, especially their parents. As children become older and more competent, the range of choices can be widened and they can be genuinely consulted about their priorities and preferences.

Although children and adults with profound and multiple impairments may not contribute to international and national meetings, it is important not to underestimate the extent to which they stand to benefit from policies and practices which emphasize choice and decision-making. Even if they cannot speak, they can often understand what is said by others and also develop other means of expressing choices and decisions, for example by physical expressions, through the voice, by means of the eyes and in many other ways personal to the individual but understandable by others.

Collaboration between Parents and Teachers

Collaboration between parents and teachers is therefore essential to such developments. Each has an important contribution to make, from their own distinctive perspectives and experiences.

All schools express a commitment to the growth of independence and autonomy of their pupils and most would agree that this includes providing opportunities for choice and decision-making. But the curriculum is often so crowded that these opportunities may be overlooked or may receive lower priority than teachers and parents would wish. For this reason, it is important that schools plan and develop a self-advocacy curriculum, under whatever name, and that they do so in collaboration with parents from the outset, not when the ideas have already been discussed and written down.

A self-advocacy curriculum is not a slot that appears on a timetable once or twice a week. It should inform and permeate each and every activity undertaken in the school and in the home. Whatever else is being done, the emphasis should be on providing constant opportunities for choice and decision-making by the child. A videotape or observation of any classroom or home activity will indicate how many such opportunities have in fact been made available. Parents and teachers can then compare notes and exchange ideas and experiences.

Opportunities for choice and decision-making should therefore be at the heart of all the activities of the school and should be seen as a central element of the policy of the school. In one sense, this applies to all children and all schools, whether ordinary or special. In some ways it is easier to do this in a special school, partly because the philosophy is likely to be acceptable and partly because smaller classes and better staffing ratios make it easier to implement. But even in an ordinary class of 30 children, a good teacher will try to ensure that each child will have opportunities for decision-making.

Despite a crowded and prescriptive National Curriculum, teachers in the UK have tried to ensure that 'an empowerment curriculum' is retained (Coupe O'Kane and Smith, 1994). Sebba *et al.* (1993) argue that personal and social education in the widest sense should be at the heart of the curriculum while still remaining within the official National Curriculum. Here again, partnership with parents is an essential, though often overlooked, element of success.

The Appendix to this chapter includes a number of suggestions for ways in which schools can promote self-advocacy, based on work by Pam Gunton (1990), as part of a course at Cambridge University Institute of Education. The extracts are mostly taken from the 'general philosophy' introduction to her paper. But many concrete and specific examples are also included which are relevant to specific areas of the curriculum, such as language and communication, music, dance, physical education and games. Many examples are also given of ways in which opportunities for choice and decision-making can be given to children with profound and multiple learning difficulties as well as those with very limited communication skills.

I would only add that parents should be involved in the development of such a programme from the outset and encouraged to make suggestions on how it can be implemented equally in the home and at school. Success depends on complete partnership between home and school. Each is indispensable to the other.

Conclusions

The self-advocacy movement is a reality and is likely to grow in strength and in the nature of the demands which it makes. It should be supported and encouraged by professionals, by voluntary organizations and by the authorities.

The attitudes and feelings of families towards self-advocacy organizations and the self-advocacy activities of their sons and daughters will differ from family to family. Some families may experience difficulties and doubts about the implications of adult status; there may be conflicts and communication problems within the family, just as there are in other families. These can often be resolved within the family but support from outside can also be helpful.

Families who have good experiences in working collaboratively with professionals are likely to have had opportunities to discuss self-advocacy issues and to have been involved in a joint approach with teachers and others in providing opportunities for choice and decision-making. This is not an insurance policy against the occurrence of conflicts and problems, but at least effective foundations will have been laid at an earlier stage.

Professionals working in services, as well as members of voluntary organizations, need to be ready to lend their support in such situations but may themselves need some training in support, as considerable sensitivity is needed in working with families in difficult circumstances. There are no ready-made solutions to issues surrounding conflicts over independence and self-advocacy. Each family's needs are unique.

The training of professionals needs to pay more attention to issues arising out of the self-advocacy movement and to ways of supporting families, including the person with a learning difficulty, in making the adjustments which will be needed to work through the changes of moving towards adult status. Families themselves need more support in preparing their son or daughter for such status.

What is needed, then, is a complete reappraisal of attitudes and working relationships between parents and professionals (Mittler, 1995). Every school and every service for young people and for adults could usefully examine its policy and practice in relation to parents and in

12

particular develop new patterns of partnership and collaboration in helping people with learning difficulties reach the goal of maximum autonomy and independence.

References

Coupe O'Kane, J. and Smith, B. (eds) (1994) *Taking Control: Enabling people with learning difficulties*, London: Fulton.

Crawley, B. (1988) *The Growing Voice: A Survey of self advocacy in adult training centres in Great Britain*, London: Campaign for People with Mental Handicap.

Gunton, P. (1990) 'Encouraging Self Advocacy From an Early Age', Based on a dissertation prepared for Cambridge University Institute of Education.

Lodge, M. and Lodge, C. (1994) 'Promoting self regulation for people with learning difficulties', in Coupe O'Kane and Smith, *op cit.*

Mittler, P. (1995) 'Rethinking partnerships between parents and professionals' *Children and Society*, 9, 3, 22–40.

Sebba, J., Byers, R. and Rose, R. (1993) *Redefining the Whole Curriculum for Pupils with Severe Learning Difficulties*, London: Fulton.

Winup, K. (1994) 'The role of a student committee in promotion of independence among school leavers', in Coupe O'Kane and Smith, *op cit.*

Further Reading

Flynn,M. and Ward, L. (1991) 'We can change the future', in Segal, S. and Varma, V. (eds) *Prospects for People with Learning Difficulties*, London: Fulton.

Mittler, P. and Mittler, H. (1994) *Families and Disability*. International Year of the Family Occasional Paper No. 10, Vienna: United Nations

Sutcliffe, J. (1990) *Adults with Learning Difficulties: Education for choice and empowerment*, Buckingham: Open University Press.

Wertheimer, A. (1989) *Self Advocacy and Parents: The impact of self advocacy on the parents of young people with disabilities*, London: Further Education Unit.

Williams, P. and Shultz, B. (1982) *We Can Speak for Ourselves*, London: Souvenir Press.

Appendix I: Extract from Gunton (1990)

General Philosophy

Pupils should be treated with respect and dignity at all times. No one should be discussed or spoken about as if they were not there.

Aim to provide CHOICE whenever you can. Introduce option afternoons if you haven't already got them. Try to give choices within each lesson – choice of partner, choice of activity, choice of teacher. Don't end up with an identical object for each child at the end of the lesson. ENCOURAGE INDIVIDUALITY.

ASK THE CHILD TO MAKE DECISIONS – AND ACT ON THEM. Reasons should always be given to and asked from a pupil.

Pupils should be given every opportunity to learn that actions have consequences and that they should be able to question another's actions and explain their own.

The pupil should be asked for his/her opinion whenever possible. The fact that one's opinion is sought and acted upon helps to promote self esteem. Imagine how it would feel if no one ever consulted you about anything. Discuss feelings, preferences, whenever you can. Let pupils know you are interested in their opinions, that they matter.

Pupils should be involved wherever possible. Decisions involving pupils should be made by them if at all possible. Ask them if they would prefer a disco or a film at the end of term; hot dogs or beef burgers at the fete; where would be the best place for the new fish tank; should they have fish or terrapins?

Pupils should be allowed to make MISTAKES.

Pupils should be involved in the SCHOOL ORGANISATION. The school is there for the benefit of the children and their parents. Pupils should feel that the school is theirs and that they have a say in what goes on and what goes where. Where shall we put this display? Which flowers shall we buy for the entrance? What colour curtains, cushions?

Pupils should be given the skills to make decisions.

Carefully graded decision making should be part of every child's programme – no matter how limited their ability.

Every member of staff, every student and every volunteer should have the philosophy of self advocacy, choice and decision making explained to them.

Every parent should be told that this is the philosophy of the school. Parents sometimes need help and encouragement to allow their child to experiment and take risks. They need to be assured that their worries and desires will be taken into account and that they will always be welcomed and kept informed'.

Part 1

A Positive Approach to Sexuality for Whom?

CHAPTER 1

Getting the Balance Right

Maggie Bowen

Introduction

This chapter will begin by reflecting on changes in attitudes towards the status of people with severe learning disabilities (SLD) in our society. On the surface, it appears that some of these positive attitudes are apparent when issues relating to sexuality of people with SLD arise. However, on closer examination, there is often a mismatch between the perceived needs and the actual needs of the person with SLD

Over the last three decades the change in attitudes towards the place of people with SLD within the mainstream of society has been reflected in the nature of legislation related to public welfare and education and in an increased awareness in the principles of normalization (Wolfensberger, 1982) and the importance of equal opportunities. Educationally, The Handicapped Children Act (1970) was highly significant, since it recognized that all children regardless of their disability were entitled to educational provision. Just over ten years later, the 1981 Education Act was advocating not only education but integrated educational opportunities, although the provisos within the Act were tokenistic rather than realistic in that it is difficult to provide quality educational opportunities without additional expenditure (Bowen and Thomson, 1992). The 1988 Education Reform Act acknowledged the fact that there should be a common curriculum for all and therefore gave pupils with SLD further opportunities to be part of the mainstream system. It also encouraged educators within segregated special schools to work alongside mainstream educators; each benefiting from the expertise of the other.

Since the right to education in general is a relatively recent provision for people with SLD, it is not surprising that discussions about the relevance of a sex education programme for them is sometimes disputed. The subject is a contentious one for everyone and that is why it is an issue that has a prominent place in educational legislation and the media. Many of you may recall, for example, the incident reported in the press about the school nurse in Leeds who had answered questions asked of her about sexual matters openly and frankly (Young, 1994). Some of the parents of the junior-age pupils involved in the lesson were so outraged that the event even prompted a response from the Minister of Education, John Patten. He is reported to have said in a TV programme, following this event, that sex education for children attending primary schools may need further consideration. (Circular 5/94, DfE, 1994, issued after the event suggests that the implementation of a sex education programme in the primary sector should be at the discretion of the school governors.) I wonder how much more publicity this event might have had had it happened in a school for pupils with SLD?

Parents and professionals, as aforementioned, have for some years now played an active role in deciding to what extent sex education should be taught in our schools. For example, although the 1986 Education Act gave school governors the ultimate responsibility to produce a written statement about the content and manner of delivery of the curriculum in this area, in theory, it also increased parental responsibility as a result of some parents being parent governors and all parents being given the opportunity to attend annual meetings with governors. The 1988 Education Reform Act emphasized the responsibility of schools to prepare pupils for the opportunities and responsibilities of adulthood. The 1993 Education Act qualifies the responsibility of teachers and governors by giving parents the right to withdraw their child from all or any part of a sex education programme. In other words, though schools are responsible for producing a programme of sex education for pupils, it is up to parents to decide whether or not they wish their offspring to benefit from such provision. So parents, not governors, are now the people ultimately in control of sex education in our schools.

Such legal requirements intensify the problems that parents in particular, but also teachers, governors and carers face in deciding, for example, the answers to the following questions:

- Should schools be involved in the sex education of pupils with learning difficulties?
- If they should, how should they approach sex education with pupils who have learning difficulties?
- What should children with learning difficulties be taught about sex; and how should they be taught?
- When and where should sex education begin? How should it be conducted?
- Who should be involved?

Professionals and carers face a number of dilemmas when confronted with the developing sexuality of the young people with whom they are living and working. Those who care for and about people with learning difficulties want to do what's best for them (Fairbairn and Bowen, 1993a). But, like us all, they are limited by their background, by their values and experiences, by their understanding and by their hopes and fears. Many parents, carers and staff and even the government recognize the need for sex education in our special schools (Circular 5/94, DfE, 1994) and the importance of coming to terms with the fact that children with SLD grow and develop into adults just like the rest of us. The following stories, most of which are real and all of which will have a familiar ring to them, examine a number of relationship issues. They illustrate the desire to do what is best, what is just and what seems to be the most respectful of the person with SLD. Sadly though, they will also show that this is not achieved as easily as first anticipated.

Geraint and Huw

Geraint (aged 14) and Huw (aged 10) attend a residential special school. Despite the age gap between them, they had always been good friends and their friendship was encouraged when they were given the opportunity to share a bedroom. Their friendship flourished until some months later staff began to notice that they could not be found during break times. When this was investigated, it was discovered that the boys were spending break times behind some bushes at the bottom of the school field. The staff thought nothing of this and were in fact delighted that the boys' friendship was continuing to blossom.

But then one day after break Huw arrived in class looking flushed and tearful. Later on that day he broke down and cried bitterly but would not say what was wrong. Eventually, however, he told staff that Geraint was constantly bullying him. He also told staff that Geraint liked to touch his 'willy' and now it was very sore.

A case conference was held with both sets of parents present and it was decided that both boys should receive 'counselling' and that Geraint should no longer be allowed to attend school as a boarder.

What are your opinions about this case? Would you have handled it in the same way? What do you think would happen in the counselling sessions the boys were supposed to have? Sometimes such 'counselling' consists of little more than the boys being told what they must and must not do or what their rights are, rather than involving any attempt to look into the problem more deeply or even, in the case of the abused child, to offer any help in coping with the anxiety that he had been caused.

In incidents of this kind, it is often the case that both staff and parents engage in crisis management. Though at the point of crisis they do what they consider to be best for the young people who are involved, it is arguably the case that they end up looking to the most obvious solution which is often not the most helpful in the long term. Suspending Geraint from the residential part of the school will not prevent him having access to Huw during the day. After all, most of the abuse inflicted on Huw occurred during daytime breaks and even if staff were particularly vigilant in seeing that the two boys were kept apart, it would always be possible for Geraint to find some other vulnerable child with whom to engage in sexual activities. What is more, he might find some younger child who would enjoy the activity so much that he would keep quiet about it or be unable to communicate about it. Once again, are we witnessing temporary prevention rather than a long-term solution?

In a situation like that in the story of Geraint and Huw, the question also arises as to whether Geraint has learned about homosexual activity through some experience he has had. Perhaps he is a homosexual or maybe he is just exploring his sexuality with whomever he can gain access to. If he was getting a thrill and excitement from his experience with Huw how did staff intend to help him to divert his attention in a more acceptable way? Many questions of this nature need to be addressed if the real and underlying problems are to be solved. Because this is not a nice, possibly a shocking event to deal with, intervention has been abrupt in the hope that the problem will go away and not return.

Sarah

Sarah had always had plenty of affection in her life. Despite the fact that she was wheelchair-bound she had always had the opportunity to go to plenty of places, using a computer aid to communicate her needs and converse with people. She was a talented and likeable young girl.

When she was 16, Sarah became very depressed; she did not want to go out and she became withdrawn. Eventually, Sarah confessed that she was unhappy because she had realized that she was different from other teenagers; she went to places but was not likely to meet a boyfriend. Staff at school introduced Sarah to a wheelchair-bound boy thinking that with a common disability they would undoubtedly get on.

Staff acted in good faith to help a young lady that they were fond of. However, two questions can be raised. First, didn't the staff make certain assumptions and second, why wasn't Sarah's desire to be an adolescent recognized earlier by adults who no doubt knew her well? Fortunately Sarah's story had a happy ending: she and her boyfriend Marc spent many years together, eventually ending up in a community placement. But was it luck or good judgement that brought about Sarah's happiness?

John

John's parents acknowledged the fact that he was now reaching adulthood as a 17-year-old (Fairbairn and Bowen, 1993b). Realizing that he was growing into an adult and should have the opportunity to mix with other adults, his mother began taking him with her to coffee mornings and whist drives at church, while his dad occasionally took him to the pub or to football matches. They did not, however, encourage John to spend time with his friends from school or even to join in any of the activities in the neighbourhood in which other adolescents tended to engage, such as youth clubs. Indeed, on the few occasions that John was invited to spend time with friends of his own age, his parents always managed to have an alternative activity available that they thought he would enjoy more.

It could be argued that by not encouraging him to develop interests outside the family, John's parents were failing to acknowledge his needs as an adolescent. This is not to say that they intended to do so; no doubt they were doing their best to involve him in adult activities, encouraging him to grow up. And yet it could be argued they were denying him the experience of average adolescent boys, for example, discos, youth clubs and mixing with the opposite sex. It could be argued that by failing to support John's requests to be allowed to go and spend time with others on occasions when he was invited to do so, they were denying him the opportunity to develop the ability to make informed choices between the coffee mornings and the pub and the football with dad, and the alternative age-appropriate activities in which he might have engaged.

John's story is an example where it is at least arguable, perhaps even likely, that his caring parents misjudged what was best if they wanted to help their adolescent son to grow up, develop adult interests and nurture peer group friendships. On the surface, there seems to be nothing about his parents' behaviour to suggest that sex played any part in their deliberations and decisions about how to act. However, it might well have been the case that at a subliminal level, their reason for keeping John close to home where possible, stemmed from misgivings relating to his obvious sexual maturity; for example, about what he might do, or what might happen to him, if they were not with him.

David

David was 16, hyperactive and, although likeable, prone to violent outbursts. He had lived with his mother only since he was four and during the early years of his life witnessed his father beating his mother. Concern was also expressed at this time by members of the Pre-School Playgroup Association that David was being sexually abused by his paternal uncle, although little or nothing was done about it. David had always behaved offensively towards others. Sometimes he pulled up girls' dresses and hugged, grabbed and kissed males and females indiscriminately when he felt the urge. The behaviour worsened, the staff insisted, when David reached puberty. At all times when this happened staff simply said, 'Naughty, David' and encouraged him to shake hands. They believed that David had always been starved of affection and so disliked the idea of denying him physical contact with others.

David's story highlights a number of issues. First, why wasn't he taught at a young age how to show his affection towards people in a socially acceptable way? Second, if abuse was suspected and it was known that David saw violence in his home, should he have been given some help so that he could get such abusive behaviours into perspective? Finally, was he aware that pulling up girls' dresses had sexual connotations or was he simply seeking attention in what always had been an effective way? Sadly, David's problems were only addressed when he became of an age and size that they could no longer be overlooked. At this stage it was no longer possible to treat the behaviour as either cute or amusing. All too often, problems of this nature i.e. anti-social sexual behaviours, are swept under the carpet until the time comes when they cannot be ignored because the perpetrator is no longer an easily dismissed, excusable child. It is often difficult for those involved with pupils with SLD to look forward to the latter's adulthood because the problems that need facing are too difficult to come to terms with. However, if David's growing up had been recognized and planned for, perhaps his carers would not have had to deal with problems of anti-social, offensive behaviour in adulthood.

Mandy

Mandy attended a mainstream school part time (Fairbairn and Bowen, 1994). She had severe learning difficulties and exhibited challenging behaviour. She was a capable student, provided she was constantly supervised on a one-to-one basis. However, if left unsupervised, Mandy abused herself her by biting her hands and pulling her hair and as a result her hands were kept bandaged at times. In addition to these behaviours there were other problems: Mandy was aggressive towards and often kicked and punched others. Mandy had other behaviour patterns which staff found even more difficult to deal with. In particular she frequently exposed herself. This was undignified for her and offensive to others. As a result, the decision was taken that she should wear trousers rather than a skirt at school, even though standard school uniform for girls was a skirt. This helped to some extent, because of the difficulty Mandy experienced in removing her trousers without assistance.

When Mandy started her periods she became extremely distressed and aggressive when she saw the blood. After the onset of periods, her challenging behaviour worsened very noticeably. She objected to having to wear sanitary towels and managed to discard them in spite of the difficulty she experienced in removing her trousers. The desire to remove sanitary towels consequently led to an increase in her exposing behaviour. Her self-harming behaviour also increased during her periods and, on one occasion, she banged her head so hard against the wall, that it was feared that she had fractured her skull.

Seeing Mandy so distressed caused significant others in her life a good deal of pain. They have always endeavoured to make Mandy's life as normal as possible and found her self-harming behaviours particularly difficult to cope with. Mandy was therefore taken into hospital for a hysterectomy in the hope that the problem would go away.

Mandy's case raises a number of issues. Since it could be argued that this is a situation where physical welfare is also at stake, was a hysterectomy the best course of action? How could it be considered abusive, it might be asked, to do what one could to help someone about whom one cares, to overcome a problem which is now affecting all aspects of her life for one week in every four and preventing her from leading a happy life with her mainstream peers?

However, other less drastic things could, of course, have been done for Mandy. For example, behavioural therapy can be very successful in dealing with self-mutilating behaviours. Or perhaps a behavioural programme could be combined with a more educational course of action designed to help Mandy, as far as possible, to come to terms with what is happening to her body. In order to facilitate this, she could have perhaps been prescribed medication to subdue her periods for a time.

It is important for everyone that Mandy should continue attending a mainstream school. If drug treatment is not possible to reduce her periods for a while, a possible short-term alternative would be that while behavioural and educational work is being carried out, she should return to her segregated special school during her periods, in order that the distressing behaviour in which she engages does not further jeopardize her position in her mainstream placement. Better still, she could be taken out of her mainstream school only during those days in her cycle when she is most likely to have difficulties.

It is hard to imagine that a hysterectomy would be the best or even a reasonable first step to take in coping either with Mandy's upset, or with her challenging behaviour. When a person is mutilating herself, drastic measures might in the end be justifiable to avoid serious physical harm. Even if they were not justifiable, it is easy to imagine a parent becoming so distraught with worry that any solution which protected her child's physical welfare and prevented social ostracism would seem worthwhile, whatever the cost.

Josie

Josie was a young woman in her late teens. She was a lively girl and been fostered since she was a baby by a Mrs Hughes. Mrs Hughes always wanted to do what was best for Josie and knew that in the course of her work at a local restaurant, Josie had met a young man, Jim, of whom she was very fond. Mrs Hughes was happy for them to go out on dates but was aware of the possibility that Josie could get pregnant, especially as Jim had a place of his own. She therefore phoned her (female) social worker and asked her if she would give Josie information and advice about taking the contraceptive pill. The social worker was happy to do this and spoke at length to Josie about the practicalities and the emotional issues surrounding her new romantic relationship.

Three months later, Mrs Hughes contacted her social worker in tears; she said that Josie had become unbearable to live with, she had broken ornaments and was refusing to go to work. When questioned about the state of Josie's relationship with Jim, Mrs Hughes replied that the affair had ended about a month ago and that she had therefore taken Josie contraceptive pills away from her.

In her desire to do what was best for Josie, Mrs Hughes had concentrated on the mechanics and practicalities involved in a romantic liaison and ignored the great emotional upheaval that romantic and sexual relationships can often bring. As in the case of Sarah, it was very easy to do what at face value seemed to be the right thing without looking to human feelings and desires, or consulting the young person in question.

Conclusion

It is likely that, as with most young people, the person with learning difficulties will also make and break relationships throughout their lives. It is important therefore that people with SLD are given appropriate information, education and counselling so as to avoid some of the situations outlined above. In the context of relationships, it is interesting to note that research undertaken by Davies and Jenkins (1994) into the social patterns of people with learning difficulties stated that half of the young people interviewed said that they had a special friend of the opposite sex, although a few of these were fantasies involving television personalities or day centre staff. It is perhaps sad to hear that nearly all of these young couples found it impossible to develop their relationship beyond the boyfriend/girlfriend stage associated with junior school days. Davies and Jenkins talk of the parents of a 21-year-old woman who are quite happy for their daughter to have a friendship 'with a little boy her own age' but not a man ten years older. Taking the previous case studies into account, it is not surprising that Davies and Jenkins' research concluded that the social life of young people with disabilities is very different from the social life of their regular peers. Socialization takes place mostly in the company of parents and their friends, and some are lucky to have the opportunity to attend a Gateway club or similar group. If special relationships are formed under such circumstances they are almost impossible to pursue.

In this particular instance and indeed in most of the case studies discussed the issue is not only one of attitude but also expectation. Where expectations are low, the person with learning difficulties is seen as someone who is incapable of decision-making and lacking in the ability to understand explanations about socio-sexual matters. So, for example, an action such as inappropriate touching may cause unnecessary problems when a person with learning difficulties reaches adulthood because it has not been dealt with appropriately in childhood. Even when expectations appear on the surface to be high, as in the case of Josie, many important underlying issues can be left unaddressed, thus causing the person concerned more harm than good. It is essential therefore that all of us living and working with people with learning difficulties think carefully about whether or not the actions we are taking in relation to their sexuality are appropriate to their needs and capabilities.

References

Bowen, M. and Thomson, J. (1992) 'Being there isn't enough', in Fairbairn, G.

24

and Fairbairn, S. (eds) *Integrating Special Children: Some ethical issues*, Aldershot: Avebury.

Davies, C. and Jenkins, R. (1994) 'Socialising: How can young adults with learning disabilities pursue special relationships?', *Llais*, 31, Winter.

DES (1978) *Special Educational Needs* (The Warnock Report), London: HMSO.

DfE (1994) Education Act 1993: Sex Education in Schools. Circular 5/94, London: HMSO.

Education (Handicapped) Children Act 1970, London: HMSO.

Education Act 1981, London: HMSO.

Education Act 1986, London: HMSO.

Education (No.2) Act 1986, London: HMSO.

Education Reform Act 1988, London: HMSO.

Education Act 1993, London: HMSO.

Fairbairn, G. and Bowen, M. (1993a) 'Sexuality, learning difficulties and doing what's right', *The SLD Experience*, 5, 7.

Fairbairn, G. and Bowen, M. (1993b) 'Learning difficulties: adolescence and the denial of adolescence', *SLD Experience*, 7, 16.

Fairbairn, G. and Bowen, M. (1994) 'Harm, self-harm and hysterectomy', *The SLD Experience*, Issue 8, 13.

Wolfensberger, W. (1982), 'Social role valorisation: a proposed new term for the principle of normalisation', *Mental Retardation*, 21, 234–9.

Young, S. (1994) 'Mars row fuels fear over censored sex classes', *The Times Educational Supplement*, 1 April.

CHAPTER 2

Sexuality and People with Profound and Multiple Impairment: A Positive Approach

Caroline Downs and Ann Craft

The Sexuality and Profound and Multiple Impairment Project

A two-year project, The Sexuality and Profound and Multiple Impairment Project, started in January 1994 and will, we hope, offer a positive approach to sexuality for many people: service users, parents, carers and staff. This project, directed by Ann Craft and coordinated by Caroline Downs, is based in the Department of Learning Disabilities at the University of Nottingham and is designed to explore safeguards, strategies and approaches relating to the sexuality of children, adolescents and adults with profound and multiple impairment.

The target population comprises all those people for whom, as yet, little research or literature, and even fewer materials, in the area of sexuality exist. A satisfactory way of describing such a disparate group of people is perhaps impossible to find. James Hogg (1991) points to the confusion over terminology which exists and which results, inevitably, in great communication difficulties within this country, let alone with colleagues in North America and Europe. For the purpose of this project, we have taken the advice of Matthew Griffiths (1991) and have adopted the term 'profound and multiple impairment', in order to acknowledge the extreme disabilities and difficulties experienced by these individuals, and also indeed by those who live and work with them, in trying to develop skills to understand and interact with the world around them. We are talking about those children and adults who have very high levels of dependence, whose communication is often called 'pre-intentional', whose social awareness, i.e. awareness of others and their surroundings, seems to be very limited and who may indeed be unaware of themselves.

When choosing the term we would employ, we resisted the inclusion of terms such as 'physical and sensory disabilities' because within this project, while many of our population do have such impairments, many do not. We are also addressing the needs of clients who have diagnoses of autism, or mental ill health; of those who appear to have withdrawn from their surroundings, and of those who may injure themselves, or be very aggressive towards others and whose behaviour presents a real challenge to their carers and teachers. The aims of the project include:

• the generation of a supportive network of and for those with responsibilities for children, adolescents and adults with profound and multiple impairment;
• an examination of the ethical, practical and managerial issues which concern carers, parents and teachers (we are using the last term to denote all people who are employed in an educational or therapeutic capacity, as distinct from a caring role);
• one or more publications offering models, strategies and approaches on themes related to sexuality identified by project groups.

The project arose largely in response to professionals' requests at dissemination workshops for a sex education package for students with severe learning difficulties, *Living your Life* (Craft and members of the Nottinghamshire SLD Sex Education Project, 1991). Repeatedly the need was expressed for a similar resource for service users with more complex disabilities, whose social and communicative difficulties preclude them from employing any of the already published materials. The needs of clients – and indeed those of the carers and teachers – which were being defined and expressed at these workshops differed widely. Consequently, when considering an appropriate methodology for this project, it was decided to adopt an action research approach, broader in scope than the strategy used to develop *Living your Life*, whereby a small group of practitioners from one locality produced materials for trial. In the current project the participants and groups are drawn from a national pool. Bids were invited from staff teams in schools, colleges, day centres and residential settings throughout Britain to take part either as 'project groups' or as 'trial groups'. The role of the project groups is to develop a pertinent area of work from one or more of the following themes:

• the personal, social and educational needs of children, adolescents and adults with profound and multiple impairment;
• the needs of their parents, carers, and teachers;
• guidelines and safeguards within institutions in which learning takes

place, and/or personal care is given, i.e. schools, day centres, residential settings and colleges.

From the many creative applications we received, 14 project groups were selected. They are, at the time of writing, exploring and developing materials and/or strategies for an aspect of sexuality which has particular relevance to them and to the students for whom they have responsibility.

Once developed, the materials will be evaluated in different settings by other 'trial' groups. In the light of the feedbacks and comments received, the original materials will be amended and refined and finally disseminated nationally through project publications.

A positive approach to sexuality for the individuals with profound and multiple impairment

The title of this project combines two concepts not generally employed together: 'profound and multiple impairment' and 'sexuality'. All too often the term 'profound and multiple impairment' will be associated with dependence, sensory impairment, incontinence, immobility, severely challenging behaviour and so on. It is our intention that this unfamiliar linguistic and conceptual association of 'profound and multiple impairment' with 'sexuality', will open our minds to a new possibility: to a new way of looking at the people with whom we work or for whom we care.

Ignoring or denying the sexuality of the individuals for whom we provide intimate personal care both prevents and protects us from having to acknowledge many difficult and painful aspects of ourselves. We will explore this notion in greater detail later in terms of the needs of parents, carers and teachers. For the time being, it suffices to recognize that ignoring or denying the sexuality of the individuals with profound and multiple impairment inevitably shapes and limits our expectations of them and thus their potential learning and development. Reaching the position where we are able to acknowledge the fact that, as human beings, our students/clients are by definition sexual beings, opens up new possibilities. For example, if we deny or choose to ignore a student's or client's sexuality, their masturbating will inevitably be seen as aberrant or as inappropriate behaviour. Naturally we will then be looking for medical, quasi-medical, or behavioural causes and 'solutions' to the situation. It is, of course, important to be sure that an individual who masturbates frequently is not, in fact, suffering from some sort of physical discomfort, or from the side effects of medication on the one hand, nor being reinforced by large amounts of attention contingent on self-stimulatory behaviour on the other. However, by fixating on medical or behavioural explanations and 'problems', we will inevitably deny or ignore the sexuality of our students and we will consequently stop looking at the whole person. If, on the other hand, we acknowledge the sexuality of our client/daughter/son, masturbation becomes quite natural and understandable (as is, of course, not masturbating!) Our responses are thereby extended beyond checking her or his pad is not too tight, or ensuring that she or he is constantly occupied, towards seeking to promote the sensuality and sexual well-being of these individuals and hence to a very different set of responses.

It is to be hoped that the pairing of the terms 'sexuality' and 'profound and multiple impairment' will provide an association which will open up new perspectives and, therefore, approaches. It allows for, and indeed encourages, wider definitions of sexuality as we are prompted to explore beyond the narrow, rigid image reinforced by society, namely that the only sexuality worthy of respect or acknowledgement is heterosexual intercourse within a stable relationship. We start to look at a more open-ended concept of sexuality which enables individuals' horizons to be extended and to have their needs met as a child, adolescent and adult. The project takes for its definition of sexuality the wide interpretation of Breuss and Greenberg (1981), which embraces the biological, moral, psychological and social components of sexuality. We, as parents, carers and teachers, are thereby freed to view the sexuality of our offspring/clients/students both in terms of physical growth and their resulting needs and as unique emotional, social, sexual and psychological adjustments to their environment and experiences. The more we know and understand about the individual's perceptions and life encounters, the more we will understand her or his social and emotional needs and the resulting sexual behaviour. Within this context we have identified the following as the major areas of focus for the project:

- teaching strategies and methods for developing learning opportunities and experiences about: body awareness, self-concept, relationships and social opportunities, the communication of feelings, needs, wants, the expression of likes and dislikes and self-advocacy. This includes the consideration of how staff come to decisions regarding priorities, aims, processes and activities for their students/clients;
- an exploration of how we may become more skilful at recognizing and understanding our clients' communications;
- an exploration of how parents, carers and teachers approach interactions relating to sensual pleasure and touch, health care, intimate personal care tasks, emotional well-being, personal and sexual safety. These include looking at how we may provide an ethos of

dignity and respect, and how this can be reflected in clothing, self-presentation and environment;

• ways of improving our skills in communicating concepts to the people with whom we live or work.

We know that an infant's disabilities may affect the early bonding detrimentally which may, in turn, adversely influence his or her relationships in later life. Blindness, for example, may deprive the care-giver of the feedback she or he is expecting and requires from the baby; the alternative responses of a blind infant may need to be explained to a care-giver in order that she or he receives the satisfaction needed to maintain and develop the bonding process. A slow response from the infant can subvert the turn-taking process which underpins communication, resulting in the parent dominating rather than facilitating an interaction. Inevitable feelings of guilt, disappointment or ambivalence on the part of the parent if these are not resolved or contained or redirected in some way will also adversely affect the quality of the relationship, and the bonding process.

The philosophy of normalization (Wolfensberger, 1972) which, although less predominant than in the last decade, continues to influence services for people with learning difficulties, stresses the 'ordinariness' of the issues of the people with whom we work. There are times, however, when the common (mis)interpretation of normalization is disadvantageous for our students/clients with profound and multiple impairment, as we accordingly deny either the different needs people may have, or the necessary 'extraordinary' means of meeting the same or similar needs – or indeed both. As staff, it is our duty to extricate ourselves from the prevailing attitudes and beliefs and culture of a non-handicapped society which is so pervasive and deeply entrenched that it feels 'natural'. It is our task to see beyond and behind our reinforced beliefs, and to see and value difference, where this exists, simply and impartially as *difference*, and to acknowledge and explore how we can balance our obligation, as a member of staff, to support an individual to 'fit in' with societal norms and demands with our conflicting role of changing society to accommodate an individual with unusual or challenging behaviour.

The sexual needs of our students may often differ from those of the majority. In one early study, for example, Wendy Greengross (1976) found that some of the young adults with severe learning difficulties with whom she worked, seldom wanted intercourse, but rather gentle contact – cuddling and sleeping together for warmth and comfort. The narrowly defined images of sexuality to which we are daily exposed – of glowing health, for example, of the perfect physique, of 'natural beauty' and charm – exclude many of us from the 'club of the acceptable', with well documented detrimental effects to our self-esteem. By taking a wider view of sexuality this project includes people who would otherwise be seen as too isolated, too disturbed, too developmentally young, too physically disabled, to have their needs addressed.

On the other hand, the sexual needs and desires of our clients will often be common to all people and therefore more readily understood by us: to be loved for example, for release from sexual tension, for menstrual care and so on. However, the manifestation of these needs may be different; the means of meeting these needs will often be different, because of the degree of mental and physical impairment. For example, a client may experience sexual frustration as any other human being might. She or he may manifest it in a similar or in a different way to how most of us would – for example, by self-mutilation. Relieving the frustration generally will be carried out in a different way and will require moral decisions and creative planning, within well thought out guidelines, to ensure that the help a client may require to masturbate, for example, is delivered in the least invasive way, and with the highest degree of protection for the parties concerned.

Research tells us that the part of the brain responsible for experiencing and expressing emotions – the brain stem and the limbic system – are the parts of the brain which in people with profound and multiple impairment, are usually intact (Latchford, 1989). Recognizing the emotions expressed by our sons/daughters/students however, in a way which may be conducive to their developing intentional expression and communication, presents us with an enormous challenge. It is not uncommon, for instance, to attribute a behaviour, for example rapid breathing, a cry, a laugh, to an emotional state when, in fact, this may be a manifestation of the individual's syndrome (Coupe *et al.*, 1988).

Even when observed behaviour is correctly attributed as reflecting an individual's emotional state, discrepancies are seen between different people's interpretations of the same piece of affective behaviour. Studies of the emotions experienced and demonstrated by people with profound and multiple learning disabilities (Latchford, 1989; Withers, 1991) report the definitions given by the parents and carers of their sons' and daughters' displays of feeling. The reliability of measurement is not described however. In a current study in which methods of identification and measurement actually are identified (Hogg *et al.*, 1995), discrepancies in interpretations given by carers are noted, which casts doubt on reliability of judgement. We shall explore later the influence our own feelings may have on our individual interpretations of the feelings of other people.

Even when we are successful in being open to our students and see them looking sad or frightened, we often fail to build on these very real potential learning experiences, or even acknowledge that our client may feel that way. It is much less painful for us whose professed intention it is to make life 'better' for the people with whom we work, to see the objects of our care as happy. We often need to be thanked for our dedication and efforts with a smile, or at least to be reassured that everything is alright really. Frequently, people with physical disabilities report experiences of being pressured into taking responsibility for the feelings of a non-disabled person with whom they are interacting; being required somehow to console others that, however disabled she or he may be, life is nevertheless fine (Keith, 1994). It seems that many non-disabled people push those with disabilities into a role of purity, patience, enduring good humour and acceptance of their (often limited) lifestyle by communicating, as we do, that we do not really wish to hear about or suffer their pain, anger and frustrations. So great is our need for this reassurance from people with profound and multiple impairment, to see from them that, despite everything, they are ok, that we consequently fail to acknowledge what is really before our eyes. Exhortations such as, 'Give me a smile' and, 'Cheer up' may frequently be heard in interactions with students throughout the country.

The needs of staff and carers, in relation to promoting the sexuality of the people within their care, will be discussed in more detail below. As we start to explore this area, it quickly becomes clear that we, as staff, are in a significantly stronger position to acknowledge the feelings and sexuality of individuals with profound and multiple impairment when we develop an understanding of our own needs and deep-rooted attitudes.

A positive approach to sexuality for the parents/carers/teachers of individuals with profound and multiple impairment

Recognizing and promoting the sexuality of the extremely disabled people with whom we live or work is clearly of great importance if we are to view them as whole people, and if they are to derive the potential benefits from learning experiences of the sort outlined previously. This approach needs to rest, of course, on a philosophy which views individuals with profound and multiple impairment as people who are sexual beings with sexual needs. These needs may or may not be the same as those of the people with the power, they may or may not be expressed in a way which is familiar to, or easily understood by, us but there has to be a recognition that meeting those needs requires sensitivity, creativity, confidence and security. Policies and guidelines, which we will discuss later, will increase security and confidence. These will be empty, however, in the absence of a deeper understanding, on the part of each of us, of our motives and underlying attitudes; guidelines and policies will not override the defence mechanisms we are so adept at using unless we have first explored our unconscious values towards disability, and towards sexuality.

We can create all manner of mechanisms by which to deny the sexuality of our offspring/students, even when the evidence of it is, quite literally, before our eyes; even when, engaged in their intimate care, we are confronted daily by their adult genitalia as we change their pads and bath them. Skilfully, we may deny the obvious and keep them young, in the way we see them and interact with them. In schools, individuals with profound and multiple impairment are still often placed in a 'special care' unit catering for students of a wide age range. We therefore do not acknowledge their physical development, increasing age and the usual rites of passage, for example of moving up into the next class. Parents too often continue to think of their adolescent, even adult, son or daughter as 'the baby' of the family.

Another frequently employed mechanism for denying clients' sexuality is that of depersonalization: referring to them as 'wheelchairs' or 'non-ambulants'. We may also distance ourselves by using impersonal or medical terminology to describe their needs, wants and very personal behaviour. How often do we refer to the 'menarche' when referring to ourselves for example, or 'solo sexual activity'? We are, indeed, quite practised and skilled at finding frames of reference to distance ourselves, and protect ourselves, from the painful fact that these damaged individuals, who are so very dependent on us for all their needs are, in fact, sexual beings. If we persevere in regarding them as asexual it is less embarrassing to change their pads so, for example, a student thereby remains a mother's baby in her own mind and she does not have to face the student's puberty – another missed milestone and cause for mourning. If we convince ourselves that 'they' do not have the same feelings and emotions that 'we' have, that 'they' do not have the same need to love and be loved, or to be touched other than for purely functional purposes, we preserve ourselves from the pain that 'someone like me' has such a limited life. How often do we dare think of people with learning difficulties as lovers – currently or potentially? 'Sexually active' they may be, but not lovers.

We, whether staff or parents or carers, need to confront those feelings we generally have well tucked away and do not acknowledge – our pain, our weaknesses, our own dependence, our fears, our sexual desires, our fantasies – which can be sharply brought into focus by those of a student.

We need to bring into our awareness those things that are generally unconscious but feed the decisions we make; the attitudes and beliefs we have which dictate what seems 'natural' or self-evident to us, but which, when explored, help us to understand our behaviour and interactions with others and thereby to have greater control over our lives. Specifically, we need to be very clear about our feelings towards our own sexuality – and the source of these feelings – disability generally, the people with whom we live or work, and not least our motives for having chosen this type of work. Have we elected to work with people with disabilities because we want to feel and indeed *be* powerful? Is it that we want to champion the cause of the oppressed, and if so, why? Is it that we need to be needed? Hilary Brown (1992) suggests that the political correctness surrounding words used to describe people with disabilities reflects the negative feelings we have towards them; that we all need, on occasion, to 'police' our cruelty which would otherwise be manifested through humour or sarcasm. However committed we may have become as adults to being responsive to the needs of our clients, it is inevitable that we will carry with us negative and disturbing images from childhood of difference and handicap. Rather than attribute the devalued status experienced by people with learning disabilities to the ignorance, or the wickedness of others, Brown points to the importance of encouraging staff to own, and to explore, their early experiences of disability. Being aware of the origins of our attitudes is particularly important for those of us working with people with profound and multiple impairment; the less we understand of what an individual is communicating about her or himself, the more of ourselves, of our unconscious material, we will project onto that person, often with a detrimental effect.

Let us for a moment consider the feelings and motives of the parents of a 10-year-old girl with profound and multiple learning disabilities, as her mother (Sheila) and father (Bri) discuss their daughter, Joe (Nichols, 1967).

Sheila (to audience): 'As soon as we were admitted to the freemasonry of spastics' parents, we saw that she had even less character than the other children. So we began to make them for her'.
Bri: 'Some never really suited'.
Sheila: 'No, like the concert pianist dying of TB'.
Bri: 'Nor the girl who was tragically in love with a darkie against her parents' wishes'.
Sheila: 'That was based on "Would-You-Let-Your-Daughter-Marry-One?"'.
Bri: 'I used to like the drunken bag who threw bottles at us if we didn't fetch her gin and pipe tobacco'.
Sheila: 'But they were all too active. The facial expression wasn't right'.

Bri: 'The one that stuck is the coach tour lady ... powder pink felt hat, white gloves, Cuban heel shoes, swagger coat...'.
Sheila: 'And seasick pills in her handbag just in case there's a lot of twisting and turning'.
Bri: 'She hates foreigners...'
Sheila: 'And council houses'.
Bri: 'And shafting. She knows to her cost what that can lead to'.

If we, as staff or parents, are to avoid entering into this type of self-delusion and projection, and are to be truly sensitive and open to the communications of our offspring or clients, we need to have worked through our deep-rooted attitudes and beliefs which underpin, and dictate, our daily actions and interactions.

The development of policies and guidelines

The quality of life for the client is dependent upon the beliefs and skills of workers, and the framework in which they operate. Policies and guidelines are, as we discussed earlier, crucial. In 1982 the London Borough of Hounslow acknowledged the responsibility employers have to set boundaries around the behaviour of their employees; such guidelines protect service users to some extent although, sadly, not entirely, from intentional abuse, by spelling out the sanctions for transgressing the guidelines and from unintentional abuse, i.e. from the individual assumptions, embedded value systems and prejudices of their care-givers, and the expected practice and 'rules' with which they are obliged to comply. However, as we noted earlier, we need to acknowledge that policies alone are insufficient to counteract the pervasiveness of deleterious attitudes that have not been worked out. By specifying how to behave in certain situations, thereby taking responsibility for the staff member's behaviour and therefore the outcome of the interaction, guidelines potentially protect care-givers from allegations of abuse and thus increase their confidence to undertake intimate personal tasks or to provide certain information or treatment. The production of guidelines ensures that those people writing them, at least, discuss and give thought to issues. All too frequently, however, the resulting policies and guidelines say very little, hiding behind ambiguities such as '(un)acceptable' or '(in)appropriate', not actually providing guidance on the sexual issues with which staff have to deal. It is, of course, very difficult to make prescriptive and generalized – or generalizable – statements because of the range of variables which exist and it is therefore understandable that guidelines are often unclear. While acceptable to some staff members, the notion that 'your professional judgement' may be required in some situations (as is overtly stated in some guidelines) demands a degree of responsibility and is not sufficiently supportive or prescriptive for others. This results in some employees, who would otherwise do so, refusing to teach sex education or to provide personal care in a private setting. It is not surprising that staff become concerned and curtail massage sessions with their clients, alarmed by what they see as 'inappropriate' sexual arousal, if they have neither guidelines to adhere to nor have themselves anticipated this possibility. It is predictable that the same level of ambiguity will be reflected in practice, when a staff member says to a student who is openly masturbating, 'Do you want to go to the toilet?'.

With people with profound and multiple impairment, this level of ambiguity is not acceptable, or practicable, even if it has, apparently, been adequate for those whose learning difficulties are less severe. In terms of guidelines for staff and advice for parents, who ask very specific and highly individual questions which pertain to their adolescent or adult son or daughter, clear statements have to be made in terms of philosophy, intentions and practice and these need to be spelled out in an unambiguous way. Individuals with profound and multiple impairment present us with a challenge which, if we work hard to meet, will have great benefits for other parts of the service.

As outlined at the beginning of this chapter, the project encourages practising staff to identify the areas and situations where current guidelines, if they exist at all, leave them unsupported, and/or where they would want employers to specify the interactions and responses and initiations required. Project groups undertaking this work will, supported by project resources, face the challenge of exploring self-generated issues. These, we anticipate, will include exploring methods of assessing and evaluating the real sexual needs of the people with whom they work; understanding their own attitudes towards sex and sexuality and dealing with their feelings about intimate care, touch, sexuality and handicap; becoming very skilful in 'reading' the most minute communication of our students; being conversant with the law relating to sex and people with learning difficulties; being creative in devising the means to allow sexual expression and satisfaction for their students according to their needs, taking into account the welfare of others and the law.

The resulting guidelines and strategies and, most importantly, the documented process of their work, will then be trialled by other staff groups working in varying settings who will give feedback, suggestions for alteration and amendments. Methods of educating existing staff, and of inducting new staff into these processes and structures, also need to be explored.

With clients/students with profound and multiple impairment we, as staff, need to be proactive; we recognize the need to initiate activities and interests in other areas of the curriculum or in the daily life of our offspring/clients. Matthew Griffiths (1991) demonstrates that staff need to take a positive stance in conferring the dignity and status associated with adulthood, and in instigating the necessary interventions to this end; the same degree of proactivity is required in the area of sexuality. With people whose lives are very passive, we cannot leave aspects of their learning to chance. We are confronted by the fact (and our contingent responsibility) that it is unlikely that they will ever do anything 'private' that someone else has not instigated or at least does not know about. David Carson (1992) reminds us that failing to act in a situation where a client's life is being limited by, for example, inappropriate sexual expression, is not a neutral or safe option for staff. The law of negligence may render us liable for not intervening. Guidelines need to incorporate recommended decision-making processes, and methods of documenting the education or treatment agreed on by staff teams.

There are no simple answers; guidelines, in order to be useful, need to be based on well thought out and agreed values, informed by self-awareness on the part of the staff, by a heightened sensitivity to the communications of clients/students and the law. In this way clients themselves may be better protected from abuse stemming from the power others inevitably have over their bodies and affairs, and staff are protected from entering into dubious, undocumented practice, even where this may be motivated by high ideals.

'Tangled and fraught with difficulty' was the description given by one of the project groups to the whole area of sexuality in relation to people with profound and multiple impairment. As project groups start to explore their chosen areas of work, issues concerning ethics, intense feelings and deep-seated beliefs are arising which, although inherent in matters relating to sexuality and all students with learning difficulties, simply cannot be ignored or dealt with in an unambiguous way in the context of people with profound disability.

As a result of their extreme dependence and vulnerability, people with profound and multiple impairment are presenting us with the challenge to address issues which, we hope, will positively influence our practice with all students and clients with learning disabilities.

References

Breuss, C. E. and Greenberg, J. E. (1981) *Sex Education: Theory and Practice* Wadsworth Publishing.

Brown, H. (1992) 'Working with staff around sexuality and power', in A. Waitman and S. Conboy-Hill, (eds) *Psychotherapy and Mental Handicap*,London: Sage.

Carson, D. (1992) 'Legality of responding to the sexuality of a child with disabilities', *Mental Handicap*, 20, 85–7.

Coupe, J. Barber, M. and Murphy, D. (1988) 'Affective communication', in J. Coupe and J. Goldbart (eds) *Communication Before Speech: Normal development and impaired communication*, London: Chapman & Hall.

Craft, A. and Members of the Nottinghamshire SLD Sex Education Project (1991) *Living your Life*, Cambridge: LDA.

Greengross, W. (1976) *Entitled to Love: The sexual and emotional needs of the handicapped*, London: Malaby Press.

Griffiths, M. (1991) *Adult Status for All? Continuing education for people with profound and multiple disabilities: A discussion paper*, London: FEU.

Hogg, J. (1991) 'Developments in further education for adults with profound intellectual and multiple disabilities, in J. Watson (ed.) *Innovatory Practice and Severe Learning Difficulties*, Edinburgh: Moray House Publications.

Hogg, J., Reeves, D., Mudford, O. and Roberts, J., (1995) *The Development of Observational Techniques to Assess Behaviour State and Affective Behaviour in Adults with Profound Intellectual Disabilities, Part 2: Affective Behaviour*, Dundee: White Top Research Centre, University of Dundee.

Keith, L. (1994) *Introduction to Mustn't Grumble*, London: The Women's Press.

Latchford, G. (1989) 'Towards an understanding of profound mental handicap', unpublished Ph.D. thesis, University of Edinburgh.

Nichols, P. (1967) *A Day in the Death of Joe Egg*, London: Faber.

Withers, P. (1991) 'Assessing the response of adults with profound learning difficulties to various forms of stimulation', unpublished British Psychological Society Diploma in Clinical Psychology thesis, Leicester: BPS.

Wolfensberger, W. (1972) *The Principle of Normalisation in Human Services*, Toronto: National Institute on Mental Retardation.

CHAPTER 3

Discussion: Parental Concerns about Puberty and Sexuality in Young People with Severe Learning Disability

Ian McKinlay

Introduction

For all parents, the challenge of coping with their children's transition through puberty into adult life is demanding. When a son or daughter has a severe learning disability there is an additional dilemma as the young person is more financially and socially dependent on carers. This can be frustrating for all involved. Adult personal relationships and sexual identity are problematical. It is, perhaps, understandable that parents tend to treat their children as if they remained young and to have difficulties with shaving them or assisting them with menstrual hygiene. After all, these are physical reminders of growing up. There are issues too for other carers and school staff. These include male and female staff attending to the personal hygiene of pupils or students. Uncertainties abound concerning the content and methods of personal, social and sex education. Cultural differences need consideration in a multi-ethnic society. It is well known that families of adolescents and young adults with SLD can become isolated and stressed (Tunali and Power 1993). They are concerned about the future care of these young people (Hallum and Krumboltz, 1993; Sanctuary, 1991) and aware of their vulnerability to neglect and abuse, including sexual abuse. The following discussion is intended to contribute to the ongoing debate in each of these areas.

Onset of Puberty

Girls with Down's Syndrome begin to have periods a year earlier (aged 12 on average) than the norm for girls in general (about 13). However, there is a wide range of menarche for other girls with SLD with a typical age of 14–15 years (Evans and McKinlay, 1988). Boys with Down's Syndrome need to shave at about 15 whereas other boys with SLD begin at a wide range of ages, but typically 16–17 years old (McKinlay *et al.*, 1995). This diversity of onset of puberty suggests that personal, social and sex education has to be planned individually.

General Independence and Developmental Ability

In recent years a greater number of frail children with multiple disabilities are surviving infancy and early childhood. More will survive into adult life. Now 90 per cent of children with cerebral palsy survive childhood, though only three-quarters of immobile children with a spastic quadriparesis do so (Evans *et al.*, 1990; Crichton *et al.*, 1995).

Of young people with SLD aged 15–25 years living in the community in Salford, Manchester about 80 per cent can walk independently, just over half can talk in sentences and a further sixth have words or phrases. Over a quarter have no speech. It is exceptional for a child with SLD who can talk to be non-ambulant, whereas most who cannot talk do not walk. Nearly half are independent for toileting or will use the toilet with prompting. A third can use the toilet with supervision or help but between a fifth and a quarter have no voluntary control over continence. Just over a third are capable of washing independently, though some checking may be necessary. A further quarter can wash with supervision and help. However, nearly 40 per cent are dependent on parents and other carers for personal hygiene. Virtually all children with SLD who are independent for toileting and washing can walk and talk in sentences. Few who can walk or who have useful speech are entirely dependent on parents and carers for personal hygiene. Most of those requiring such care are non-ambulant and without speech. They, too, need to be taken into account in any discussion of puberty and sexuality.

Shaving

It is exceptional for a young man with SLD to be independent for shaving though about a third can do so with help. All of these are ambulant and able to talk in sentences. The need for shaving seems to begin later in non-ambulant men who cannot talk. However, only half of those who can walk and talk in sentences are able to assist with shaving. Current practice seems to be that about half are shaved with a wet razor and half with an electric razor. It is unusual for a young man with SLD to be allowed to grow a beard, even though behaviour problems in shaving are common and parents/carers often report some distaste for the process.

The subject of shaving seems to have been rather neglected. Few parents recall having had any advice about it and it can cause aggravation between parents. However, some practical guidelines can be gleaned from parents comments. Some have found that a re-chargeable/battery razor is more acceptable than a wet razor. Some shave their sons infrequently after trimming with scissors. If shaving is done at the same time as another family member is shaving it may be accepted more easily. The greater relaxation some young men experience in the bath or shower may allow better tolerance of shaving.

Management of Menstruation

Three-quarters of all young women with SLD are menstruating by the age of 16. Those who are not are usually non-ambulant and unable to talk. Usually young women with SLD who menstruate are aware of their periods. The usual method of sanitary protection is the use of pads. Occasionally nappies are used for young women who are also incontinent.

Most young women with SLD who can walk and talk and who menstruate are able to use pads independently, though some require checking and others can use them with supervision. However, behaviour problems are common. These include refusal to wear pads, disposal of pads in an unacceptable manner and lack of inhibition.

Parents value advice about management of menstruation. Some will also request hormone treatment (e.g., contraceptive pills) to reduce or abolish periods and occasionally hysterectomy is requested though less often than used to be the case (Shepperdson 1995). Such treatments have considerable ethical and legal implications and should only be considered if there are clinical indications such as heavy or continuous periods. Usually, help with management techniques from school staff such as teachers or the school nurse, a clinical psychologist or the community team for people with learning disability, or other parents/carers can overcome problems.

It is important to discuss menstruation and the use of pads with young women with SLD prior to the onset of periods and within the limits of their comprehension. Practice and repeated explanation will be needed. Girls can be taught to practise the use of pads before the menarche. Some mothers allow their daughters to see the way they use and dispose of their own sanitary pads and open discussion about menstrual hygiene with others who can help is valuable.

Involvement of Carers in Personal Hygiene

When young people are looked after by link families or foster parents the same quality of advice should be available as is given to biological parents. At school, in respite care and in day centres, help with hygiene should, when possible, be given by the same person, familiar to the young person and with good liaison with parents. it is preferable for shaving to be carried out by male staff, though this is not essential. Some young men at home are shaved by their mothers. Menstrual hygiene should be managed with the help of female staff. Other aspects of personal hygiene should be managed by a staff member of the same sex as the young person with SLD.

Cultural Aspects of Care

When the family of a young person with SLD comes from a minority ethnic or cultural group, their parents' wishes should be consulted fully. If necessary this should involve help from an appropriate adult interpreter. Every effort should be made to provide help appropriately so that the family has confidence in the service and support available (Shah, 1995).

Social Interaction

Only a minority of adolescents and young adults with SLD are believed by their parents to be capable of interacting appropriately with casual acquaintances. A third are described as naive, odd or passable casual acquaintances. A sixth are described as aloof or indifferent and a similar proportion are considered over-friendly with strangers.

Worry about the vulnerability of young women with SLD is well known and is justified for some. The risk of sexual abuse is much higher than for the general population. Most are supervised throughout the day however, and opportunities for abuse ought, therefore, to be prevented. There is less appreciation of parents' worries about the vulnerability of their sons with SLD. They also have much higher risk of sexual abuse than young males in general. However, most are supervised continuously.

Asked if their sons and daughters with SLD are interested in their physical appearance as adolescents or young adults, about a third of parents say that they insist on choosing their own clothes. Many are believed to be interested in their appearance in the mirror or, at least, to be aware of how they look. A few are reported to be obsessed by their appearance.

Sexual Awareness and Activity

About three-quarters of young people with SLD are believed by their parents to be aware of the difference between males and females, though, of these, two out of five are thought to be indifferent to this difference. When asked if their sons know what sex they are, about 60 per cent of parents think they do, a sixth think they do not and a quarter do not know. Three-quarters of their daughters are thought to know they are female, a tenth think they do not and about an eighth do not know.

Parents consider that about a third of their sons and daughters with SLD could become capable of a relationship with a girl or boy friend. They report that 40 per cent of their sons and 60 per cent of their daughters show little or no interest in sexual activity. This does not seem to be related to ability to walk or talk. Frequent masturbation is observed in about half the young men and in a third of the young women with SLD. Parents relate this to sexual feelings in about two-thirds of their children. It is common for families to have been embarrassed when masturbation has occurred in public. However, it is usually dealt with by encouraging privacy. Nocturnal emissions of semen or 'wet dreams' occur in some males but do not cause concern. When asked about the sex drive of their sons or daughters, about half the parents are unable to say; it is unusual for this to be perceived as high. The parents of those willing to give an opinion are evenly split between those who describe the sex drive as normal or low. Some young people are reported to show provocative behaviour. Males have pulled their pants down in the street, gone into female toilets, kissed to excess or have shown a lack of a sense of privacy when washing. Females have flaunted in front of males, been found kissing and cuddling in cupboards or have undressed in front of male family members. Some of these incidents are not so much unusual behaviour or disinhibition as a function of the high level of vigilance of caretakers or a lack of understanding of the concept of privacy on the part of the young people.

Sex Education and Knowledge

It is unusual for young people, especially young men, with SLD to understand the link between sexual intercourse and pregnancy. About a third of males and half the females with SLD know the link between pregnancy and childbirth. The better knowledge among young women may reflect greater efforts to teach them sex education than is made for young men, very few of whom know about contraception. A few young women use some form of contraception – pills or an intrauterine device.

When this is administered without informed consent it requires the most careful consideration of ethical issues. Sterilization is now considered as an assault and requests for this which have come to court have, as a rule, been refused.

In recent years there has been a greater understanding of the need for appropriate sex education for young people with SLD. Innovative techniques have included the use of videos, cartoons and models. There needs to be close collaboration with parents and, in Britain, the consent of school governors is required. Timing is, of course, an important issue. Motivation to seek sex education is higher when the young people are in their teens or early twenties than in later adult years. By that time parents may feel they have 'got away with it' and that they do not want to 'stir things up' by introducing sex education if they have not done so previously. Some of these dilemmas are discussed in the earlier chapter by Bowen.

Two-thirds of parents and daughters with SLD and about half the parents of sons with SLD are fearful of sexual relationships for these young people. They are even more reluctant to contemplate long-term relationships or marriage (Shepperdson 1995). None the less, Craft and Craft (1979) concluded their observational study of marriages in which at least one partner had a disability by observing that such marriages can succeed and bring much happiness if the right support is provided.

Some degree of personal and social education for young people with SLD is now regarded as prudent as a means of protecting against abuse and exploitation both within and outside the home. It may seem endearing that young children hug and kiss adults indiscriminately but they must learn to distinguish family from strangers or professional social contact from sexual contact. Knowing when to move on from that to teach about sexual contact requires skill and sensitivity. Lip service may be paid to the principle that sexual expression is a legitimate activity for people with disabilities but the will to facilitate this is another matter. The perceived right to a sex life may be frustrated by lack of encouragement or opportunity. This topic has been the focus of the preceeding chapter by Downs and Craft.

A proactive role in helping to overcome sexual problems has been advocated by some professionals (e.g., Blackburn, 1995; Shelton, 1992). Indeed, failing to take such a role may not be a neutral or safe option for service providers (Carson, 1992). Information is also important: contraception reduces the risk of unwanted pregnancy; the threat of HIV infection can be contained by practising safe sex. However, there is much to be learned about the context for such technical information, about relationships within which sexual activity will be tolerated or

44

encouraged, and about assistance in sexuality. The latter includes use of magazines, videos, sex aids and being taught how to masturbate.

There is no consensus on these controversial matters. A wide diversity of views exist about what is acceptable sexual behaviour in the general population and there have been considerable changes in public discussion of sexual mores in the latter part of this century. These decades have seen considerable changes in attitudes towards services for people with disabilities. In general there is a greater will to encourage freedom to enjoy adult status, to encourage development, autonomy and individuality. At the same time there are concerns about safety and protection. In regard to sexuality, practice has emphasized control to an understandable degree but more open discussion is welcome. Such a plea is not new (Craft and Craft, 1978; Evans and McKinlay, 1989).

The preceding chapters by Maggie Bowen and by Caroline Downs and Ann Craft address these matters further. The former gives several examples of current case studies to prompt readers to consider specific issues found in daily life. Downs and Craft rehearse the general issues, including the confusion of professionals and parents, ambiguities of existing advice and diversity of general attitudes to sexuality. It is one thing to raise the questions – what do I do if my massage of a pupil causes sexual arousal, or how should I respond if a student is masturbating in a public place? The answers are another matter. However, there are high hopes of specific answers from their Sexuality and Multiple Impairment Project. Though we share Carson's view that failure to facilitate sexual expression for people with disabilities may not be a soft option, how many parents in general shy away from effective sex education of their children?

References

Blackburn, M. (1995) 'Sexuality, disability and abuse: advice for life ... not just for kids!', *Child Care, Health and Development*, 21, 81–4.

Carson, D. (1992) 'Legality of responding to the sexuality of a child with profound learning disabilities', *Mental Handicap*, 20, 85–7.

Craft, A. and Craft, M. (1978) *Sex and the Mentally Handicapped*, London: Routledge and Kegan Paul.

Craft, A. and Craft, M. *(1979) Handicapped Married Couples: A Welsh study of couples handicapped from birth by mental, physical or personality disorder*, London: Routledge and Kegan Paul.

Crichton, J. U., Mackinnon, M. and White, C. P. (1995) 'The life expectancy of persons with cerebral palsy', *Developmental Medicine and Child Neurology*, 37, 567–76.

Evans, A.L. and McKinlay, I. A. (1988) 'Sexual maturation in girls with severe mental handicap', *Child: Care, Health and Development*, 14, 59–69.

Evans, A.L. and McKinlay, I. A. (1989) 'Sex education and the severely mentally retarded child', *Developmental Medicine and Child Neurology*, 31, 98–103.

Evans, P., Evans, S. and Alberman, E. (1990) 'Cerebral palsy: why we must plan for survival', *Archives of Disease in Childhood*, 65, 1329–33.

Hallum, M. and Krumboltz, J. (1993) 'Parents caring for severely disabled adults', *Developmental Medicine and Child Neurology*, 31, 98–107.

McKinlay, I. A., Ferguson, A. and Jolly, C. (1995) 'Ability and dependency in adolescents with severe learning disabilities. *Developmental Medicine and Child Neurology*, 37, 906–14.

Sanctuary, G. (1991) *After I'm Gone What Will Happen to My Handicapped Child?*, (2nd edn) London: Souvenir Press.

Shah, R. (1995) *The Silent Minority: Children with disabilities in Asian families*, London: National Childrens Bureau.

Shelton, D. (1992) 'Client sexual behaviour and staff attitudes', *Mental Handicap*, 20, 81–4.

Shepperdson, B. (1995) 'The control of sexuality in young people with downs syndrome', *Child: Care, Health and Development*, 21, 333–49.

Tunali, B. and Power, T. (1993) 'Creating satisfaction: a psychological perspective on stress and coping in families of handicapped children', *Journal of Child Psychology and Psychiatry*, 36, 6, 945–57.

Part 2
A Life which is Age-appropriate

CHAPTER 4

When Age-appropriateness isn't Appropriate

Melanie Nind and Dave Hewett

Introduction

Working together at Harperbury Hospital School we began developing intensive interaction, an approach to facilitating the social and communication development of students with severe and complex learning difficulties and challenging behaviour. Our student group comprised adults who were pre-verbal and often unable to begin to relate to others, not making eye contact and passively or aggressively rejecting the proximity of others. We began altering our curriculum, prioritizing fundamental social and communication development, and basing our approach on the processes of caregiver-infant interaction (see Hewett, 1989). We wanted to begin at the very beginning and to utilize what researchers have shown about how sociability and communication develop in the first year of life; thus we were offering the kinds of experiences found in caregiver-infant interaction. Our new curriculum focused on what we perceived to be the developmental level and needs of our students and not on their chronological ages.

We found that intensive interaction had both a cumulative effect and its own momentum. Staff found that the approach was more suited to their philosophical and political viewpoints and was less stressful and more enjoyable to be involved in than the previous more skills-based/behavioural curriculum. Students responded very positively to being offered experiences based on their own activity, preferences and tempo and that were at a level they could understand. The results were very encouraging as students who had previously been totally isolated from social contact began to take part in the interactive games, responding, reciprocating and even initiating simple sequences. Facilitating social and communication development had not been a strength of the behavioural approaches (McCormick and Noonan, 1984) and continued to be an area of difficulty with people whose intellectual impairment was severe or who experienced autistic deficits (Howlin, 1986). Intensive interaction was of interest to practitioners working with these client groups and there began a period in which many practitioners visited the school and in which we travelled around educational and social services establishments talking about the approach. Through this process we realized that for some we had broken a golden rule – that of age-appropriateness – and we found that by doing so we had engendered a certain amount of hostility and incomprehension.

We came across staff and workplaces whose primary ethic seemed to be to make their clients more acceptable to others and keeping them 'age-appropriate' at all times was central to this. In this chapter we wish to examine the origins of this intensity of commitment to age-appropriateness and how intensive interaction highlights the problems of the concept as it is currently often applied. We place age-appropriateness in the context of normalization or social role valorization (Wolfensburger, 1983) and address some of the problems of the normalization principle and practice.

Age-appropriateness – the extreme view

Many practitioners finding out about intensive interaction shared our interest in the potential of an approach based on a model which enables infants to be transformed from their largely naive and helpless state at birth to being effective communicators with vast and complex social skills at 18 months old. Many did not see a conflict between their clients chronological age and their developmental needs. For others however, there was a reluctance even to hear and see what intensive interaction was all about because it was not age-appropriate. For these practitioners, age-appropriateness had become a rule by which to measure all possible activity and that which did not measure up would not be entertained.

We entered into a period of dialogue about this. It seemed that we could not discuss intensive interaction without discussing age-appropriateness; we tried to understand the arguments as they were put to us. Generally it was argued that to offer non-age-appropriate materials or activity was disrespectful to the person with learning difficulties. To be respectful to them we should offer them *only* the materials and experiences offered to others of their age. It was argued that our clients with learning difficulties would not behave as adults unless we treated them as such. It was also argued that we have a duty to combat the societal image of people with learning difficulties as eternal children and that the best way to do this is

50

to enable society to see them behaving in an age-appropriate manner. We will address these arguments in turn.

The issue of respect is of course a fundamental one, but also a complex one whereby we cannot simply write ourselves a checklist of rules for respect. Of course we would not want to treat people with learning difficulties disrespectfully. Intensive interaction was for us all about having a high enough opinion of our students to pay them the proper attention to develop an approach which might begin to meet their needs. For the age-appropriateness extremists, the fact that what we came up with did not involve activity that was age-appropriate meant that they could not see this respect. Their criterion for respect was the narrow one based on paying attention to the person's chronological age, not in the context of other aspects of that person, but as an isolated, independent factor.

Ideas of age-appropriateness originated from the wider concepts of normalization, and for Nirje (1976) in the Scandinavian model, part of this was about making normal everyday patterns of living available in an inclusive way: opening up opportunities. It was not about denying other patterns of living and ways of doing things which might also be valuable. This is different from the argument that *only* experiences which are normal for a person's chronological age should be offered: closing down opportunities. In theory the normalization or social role valorization principles put forward by Wolfensberger and the North Americans were about offering and not imposing culturally normative experiences. In practice, however, there are numerous problems. Where is it written, for instance, that certain materials and experiences are appropriate for a 25-year-old? How are they different from those of someone of 35 or 15? Isn't it true that we arrive at things at different stages of our lives, that there are differences according to our gender, ethnicity, culture, sexuality, and life experiences generally? As human beings we are more complex than just the sum of our years, and it must be disrespectful not to acknowledge this. In other spheres we have often come to a point whereby differences are celebrated, not denied. This should apply to disability also; we should be able to see people with learning difficulties as doing things differently sometimes; not better, or worse, just differently.

As Chappell (1992) highlights in her critique of normalization, no debate remains static and there is growing recognition amongst those associated with the normalization principle that people with learning difficulties are not an homogenous group. There is also emerging some willingness to elicit the views of people with learning difficulties rather than just assuming them, though this is more difficult when people's learning difficulties are more severe. Practitioners with regimented ideas of age-appropriateness tend not to be those who have moved on in their thinking about normalization.

Moving on to the second argument and the premise that people with learning difficulties will behave as adults if we treat them as such, this must surely be confusing wishful thinking with reality. Wolfensberger's (1983) ideas on deviance have emphasized that 'how a person is perceived and treated by others will in turn strongly determine how that person subsequently behaves'. This more sociological concept has been confused with what we know from psychologists about development. It may be true to say that underestimating someone, or offering them experiences not advanced enough for them will hold them back, but there is a lack of evidence to suggest that offering experiences at an advanced level will help that person to reach that level. To the contrary, as Norris (1991) argues many interventions are 'too developmentally advanced... for optimal learning'. Psychologists like Piaget (1952) have shown that in order to facilitate learning, the gap between what is already known and what is new to be learned cannot be too big or too small. Offering someone with virtually no communication abilities the kind of verbal input offered to others in their 30s will not help that person to gain the language abilities of the average 30-year-old. Rather it will at worst confuse and alienate the learner, at best, merely pass them by. In order to treat people with learning difficulties with respect, our behaviour in relation to them must surely have to take into account their level of language development, their understanding of the social world and their emotional maturity.

The third argument is contentious as it raises the issue of societal expectations and images of people with learning difficulties and how this relates to our role as educators. Helping to make people with learning difficulties more acceptable is perhaps at the heart of concepts of age-appropriateness and normalization. These concepts fail to break with the history of putting the responsibility for acceptance on to the shoulders of the person with learning difficulties, rather than on to the general public and those doing the judging. In this way acceptance is 'possible but conditional' (Brown, 1994, p.127).

When normalization concepts are used to hide difference and to change spontaneous behaviours which deviate from the norm, they can oppress people with learning difficulties/disabilities (Corbett, 1994). There are still many practitioners who adhere to Wolfensberger's (1983) idea that people with learning difficulties are different, perceived as deviant, and stigmatized accordingly, while normalization aims to provide for them socially valued roles. As Chappell (1992, p.43) comments, 'the onus is on changing them to make them more like "normal" people, rather than on unconditional acceptance'. Indeed, Wolfensberger's concept of normalization has been criticized for its greater concern with the image of people with learning difficulties than with their individual needs (Emerson, 1992; Szivos and Griffiths, 1990).

Many of the practitioners who have challenged us most vehemently have seen their role very much as making their clients more acceptable to the rest of society. They have been unable to say where it is written that this is their function or how they know exactly what 'society' would want of people with learning difficulties. These concerns probably stem from Wolfensberger's ultimate goal of enhancing the social role of people with learning difficulties and linked to this, the goals of enhancing their social image and enhancing their competences. Wolfensberger (1983, p.238) argues that unconditional valuing of a person will not achieve these goals, instead he says, we need to work on socially valued habits as other people 'need all the help they can get to overcome these baser inclinations' to devalue and deride. These arguments are fundamentally flawed in the way in which blame is a moveable feature.

What is happening here is that able-bodied people with average intellectual capacities have established themselves as the norm, with people with disabilities/learning difficulties being defined in relation to this norm, with lesser status. As Brown and Smith (1989, p.106) put forward in the feminist critique of normalization ideology 'like women who are the *opposite* or *second* sex in relation to men, service users exist in relation to a supposed norm and are described in terms that stress their deviation from it'. It is an obvious logic to the age-appropriateness proponents that the best way to help someone with learning difficulties, is to get them to conform, to blend in with the people who carry the status of 'normal'. Wolfensberger's writings on normalization, argue Corbett and Barton (1992), have placed a responsibility on people with learning difficulties to be more 'normal' that the norm. As Brown (1994) points out, a further weakness of normalization is its failing to acknowledge that what is presented in the media as 'normal' is in fact myth.

There are also shadows here of the once-popular 'melting-pot', with its emphasis on assimilation and sameness (Abberley, 1987). We are now perhaps more ready to accept cultural difference than difference in terms of disability/learning difficulties. A major problem with altering the behaviour of people with learning difficulties to help them to 'pass' as 'normal adults' is that this will only work for some. It will actually serve to alienate further those less likely to 'pass'. By getting involved with this we fail to challenge how and by whom the status of 'normal' is assigned (see Brown and Smith, 1989). This is very pertinent to the student group with whom we were concerned and for whom intensive interaction was developed, as they really stand no chance of 'passing'. Taking away from these learners all that is child-like confuses where their lack of status comes from, and can be, like demands on people with disabilities to hide their abnormalities, chasing unrealistic, unchallenged ideals of physical perfection and competence (Abberley, 1987). Keeping all experiences age-appropriate may give people with learning difficulties outside value by keeping everything cosmetically normal, but it can also deprive them of the personal power we should really be working towards. As Brown and Smith (1989, p.113) sum up, 'normalization as an ideology fails to make explicit this tension between giving value and taking power'.

Practitioners we have debated with have often readily admitted the childish side of themselves, that they frequently engage in activities which would be judged age-inappropriate. The difference some would argue though, is that they have the understanding of societal norms not to engage in these activities at inappropriate times, thus embarrassing themselves or others in meetings or in the high street bank. The argument follows on that for people with learning difficulties, the fact that they cannot make these subtle judgements means that it is fairer if all non-age-appropriate activity is denied them. It is almost as if there is an underlying fear that if we allow age-inappropriate activity in private, it might one day emerge in public and cause humiliation and embarrassment to the practitioner. One is led to wonder then whether extreme concepts of age-appropriateness are an extension of some practitioners' need to conform. Brown (1994, p.124) explores the idea that 'when people with learning disabilities assert their rights to sexual lives they heighten their visibility rather than increase their chances of integration and acceptance'; there may be a sense in which this is also true of asserting the right to child-like behaviour.

We would support Corbett and Barton's contention that 'adulthood is a process not a state' and that it can 'be contradictory in its expression' (1992, p.24). Part of adult status is making one's own decisions, including when to work and when to play. Having the freedom to act in a childish manner is in fact an adult prerogative and there is a lot to be worked out concerning extending this right to adults with learning difficulties. This is clearly an area within normalization when normal/normative is not defined in terms of what most people do, as in the Scandinavian model, but in terms of what is socially valued, as in the North American model. Brown (1994, p.135) highlights the importance of this difference with reference to the range of opportunities which are acknowledged and supported in terms of sexual identity and activity for people with learning difficulties. When it comes to the dimension of adult/child identity and behaviour, the closing down of choice is also the impact.

Again looking under the surface of the argument, we are led to ask whether part of the problem is society's attitude to children and childishness generally. Behaving like a child may even be more of a right for adults than children. We say this because of a frequent pressure for children in some aspects of our society not to indulge their childishness, but rather to conform to adult norms of acceptable behaviour; 'act your age' more often meaning don't be the child that you are. It may be that in our struggle to increase the status of people with learning difficulties we have got lost in distinguishing them from children because generally children are not respected: they are 'social inferiors' (Kitzinger and Kitzinger, 1989, p.13). It would be more useful to challenge notions of the inferiority of children and other groups without status. We should perhaps be examining the links between status and economic independence as suggested in Chappell's (1992) materialist analysis of disability. This is not possible within the realm of normalization, however, as the principle upholds the status quo and power imbalance between people with learning difficulties and professionals (Brown and Smith, 1989; Chappell, 1992).

Extreme followers of the notion of age-appropriateness as an all-important rule by which to judge all activity have sometimes allowed their 'good intentions' to create a tyranny. By constantly referring to the measure of age-appropriateness they may be training their clients to be overwhelmingly eager to please, they may be preventing expression of feelings and needs, and they will almost definitely be reducing the personal choice of the individuals with learning difficulties. It is of great concern to us that such extreme notions of age-appropriateness are also denying people with profound and fundamental social and communication needs, access to interventions like intensive interaction, which perhaps have the greatest chance of facilitating their personal development. This is surely an example of the problem of the normalization movement that 'visions can become oppressive rather than inspiring' (Brown and Smith, 1989, p.117).

When age-appropriateness isn't appropriate

Intensive interaction has been developed for the kinds of learners who are hardest to reach and for whom other approaches have failed to have impact (Nind and Hewett, 1994). When people have multiple disabilities and profound intellectual impairment, or when they are pre-verbal or remote from other people, intensive interaction is appropriate. The practitioner using the approach modifies her or his interpersonal behaviours with, for example, exaggerated facial expression, more dramatic use of body language, repetitive, simplified language. In this way the learner's attention is captured and held in short bursts of playful sequences. Care-givers have intuitive abilities, triggered by their infants, to adjust themselves and their games to optimize the likelihood of the infants getting involved and interested. Intensive interaction attempts to learn from this, to release these abilities in practitioners and to explore the potential of combining innate abilities to interact with an intellectual analysis of the process. It would seem contradictory to this natural model to try to adapt the activities to be age-appropriate. The understandings we gain from the research into the care-giver–infant interaction process indicate that it is the whole complex process that facilitates such rich development at such a pace. There are obvious limitations to interventions based on just elements of the process and to attempt to make the interactions age-appropriate would be to miss the point completely.

Intensive interaction starts where the learner is, geographically, emotionally and psychologically (Nind and Hewett, 1994). The more sophisticated partner adjusts her or himself to become understandable, interesting and engaging for the less able person. Part of this can be seen as joining the person in their world, perhaps sitting on the floor, perhaps reflecting back in a playful, exaggerated manner their expressions and movements. It is about the practitioner doing the adjusting, taking responsibility for establishing some mutuality and mutual pleasure through which they can enjoyably move on. It is not about the person with all the learning to do being required to make huge leaps into advanced and complex behaviours. In intensive interaction individuals with learning difficulties are already accepted and valued just the way they are; they do not have to change in order to gain our respect (Nind and Hewett, 1994). This is in contrast to some proponents of age-appropriateness who require people with learning difficulties to change their behaviour in order to gain status and respect from them.

Intensive interaction seeks to actively engage the learner in the learning process. The interactions involve the practitioner in constantly scanning for signals of feedback in extremely fine-tuned non-verbal communication. The practitioner responds to feedback by constantly adjusting the content, mood and pace of the activity to maintain optimal levels of interest and arousal. In this way the learner, however severe the learning difficulties, shares control over the activity and has an impact on how it develops (Nind and Hewett, 1988). We see this process as highly respectful, befitting the person's adult status and true to the principles of facilitating self-advocacy abilities.

When talking to practitioners about intensive interaction, we have always made explicit that we are not saying that we should treat our adult

56

learners with learning difficulties as babies; we recognize and respect their chronological age and life experiences. What we stress, however, is that we can learn from how infants learn about sociability and communication, and it makes sense to use the strategies that are most successful at their developmental stage (see also Watson and Knight, 1991). Looking at our students as whole people with different needs, we need to look at what is appropriate for their emotional, social and intellectual 'age' and not just their chronological age. If they have yet to develop the fundamentals of social and communication development, all other learning will be hampered until these needs are addressed. It is clear to us here that age-appropriateness is not appropriate as a guiding force in these circumstances. Empowerment and respect are better achieved by having a less rigid and more critical response to normalization.

References

Abberley, P. (1987) 'The concept of oppression and the development of a social theory of disability', *Disability, Handicap & Society*, 2, 5–20.

Brown, H. (1994) '"An ordinary life?": a review of the normalisation principle as it applies to the sexual options of people with learning difficulties', *Disability & Society*, 9, 123–44.

Brown, H. and Smith, H. (1989) 'Whose "ordinary life" is it anyway?', *Disability, Handicap & Society*, 4, 105–19.

Chappell, A.L. (1992) 'Towards a sociological critique of the normalization principle', *Disability, Handicap & Society*, 7, 35–51.

Corbett, J. (1994) 'A proud label: exploring the relationship between disability politics and gay pride', *Disability & Society*, 9, 343–58.

Corbett, J. and Barton, L. (1992) *A Struggle for Choice: Students with special needs in transition to adulthood*, London: Routledge

Emerson, G. (1992) 'What is normalization?', in Brown, H. and Smith, H. (eds) *Normalization: A reader for the nineties*, London: Tavistock/Routledge.

Hewett, D. (1989) 'The most severe learning difficulties: does your curriculum "go back far enough?"', in Ainscow, M. (ed.) *Special Education in Change*, London: David Fulton and Cambridge Institute of Education.

Howlin, P. (1986) 'An overview of social behaviour in autism', in Scholper, E. and Mesibov, G.B. (eds) *Social Behaviour in Autism*, New York: Plenum Press.

Kitzinger, S. and Kitzinger, C. (1989) *Talking with Children: About things that matter*, London: Pandora.

McCormick, L. and Noonan, M.J. (1984) 'A responsive curriculum for severely handicapped preschoolers', *Topics in Early Childhood Special Education*, 4, 79–96.

Nind, M. and Hewett, D. (1988) 'Interaction as curriculum: a process method in a school for pupils with severe learning difficulties', *British Journal of*

Special Education, 15, 55–7.

Nind, M. and Hewett, D. (1994) *Access to Communication: Developing the basics of communication with people with severe learning difficulties through intensive interaction*, London: David Fulton.

Nirje, B. (1976) 'The normalization principle', in Kugel, R. and Shearer, A. (eds) *The Principle of Normalization in Human Services*, Toronto: National Institute on Mental Retardation.

Norris, J.A. (1991) 'Providing developmentally appropriate intervention to infants and young children with handicaps', *Topics in Early Childhood Special Education*, 11, 21–35.

Piaget, J. (1952) *The Origins of Intelligence in Children*, New York: International Universities Press.

Szivos, S.E. and Griffiths, E. (1990) 'Consciousness raising and social identity theory: a challenge to normalization', *Clinical Psychology Forum*, 11–15.

Watson, J. and Knight, C. (1991) 'An evaluation of intensive interaction with pupils with very severe learning difficulties', *Child Language Teaching and Therapy*, 7, 310–25

Wolfensberger, W. (1983) 'Social role valorization: a proposed new term for the principle of normalization', *Mental Retardation*, 21, 234–9.

CHAPTER 5

Ages and Stages. What is Appropriate Behaviour?

Jill Porter, Nicola Grove and Keith Park

Introduction

This chapter sets out to explore the concept of age-appropriate behaviour and the subtle interactions between the way we behave and the way others behave to us. Our behaviour is partly a response to how others treat us, conversely, others respond partly on the basis of our behaviour. We investigate the nature of this process to highlight some of the ways in which schools may help or hinder the development of age-appropriate behaviour.

We start by defining appropriate behaviours as occurring when there is an approximate match between society's expectation and the individual's responses for a given context. Other writers have adopted a similar definition. Matson *et al.* (1993), for example, refer to 'socially normative' behaviour, 'consistent with same age peers' and, 'engaging in activities similar to peers'. Society's expectations are of course influenced by gender and culture as well as age. Behaviour is judged to be inappropriate when these expectations are violated, where there is a gap between the expected and the actual. Society tends to treat people who transgress in this way with less respect. Given the socially constructed nature of this definition, one option in the longer term is to try and change the attitudes of society in order to close this gap. In reality, however, there will always be occasions when there is a mismatch between the expectations of society and the behaviour of particular individuals. It is this mismatch which is addressed in the following pages.

Characteristically discussion of age-appropriate behaviour elicits a discussion of what is, or what is not, age-appropriate. Behaviour is not however easily classified in this bipolar way. We do not for example go directly from exhibiting child-like behaviour to adult behaviour, and at least during the early teenage years there may be quite inconsistent behaviour, with teenagers varying from day to day and activity to activity in the degree to which they appear adult-like in their responses. (It is likely that there is also inconsistency in the expectations of others, leading to varying expectations and types of treatment.) Even during adulthood we do not totally abandon child-like behaviours. Mostly, however, we are quite selective about when and where we display these behaviours. We may, for example, confine these 'outbursts' to situations when we are alone or with close family and friends. On occasion these immature behaviours may be emitted in less appropriate situations when perhaps we are experiencing strong emotions, of pleasure, anger or frustration. Clearly then, even when reaching maturity, we don't uniformly adopt adult behaviours but we are largely able to discriminate between situations where the tolerance level is reasonably high and those where it is not. Not only do we perceive the time and place for different behaviours but probably more importantly, we display these disparate behaviours in moderation, for example by limiting their duration. Only occasionally, often when emotions are running high, do we depart from this. It is important to remember these aspects when we start to consider the behaviour of people with severe learning difficulties, whether they are children, teenagers or adults.

One reason why we may regulate our own behaviour is that we recognize the link between what we do and the way others treat us. We are aware that other people quickly form impressions of us based, at least initially, on our overt behaviour. This initial impression may serve to prolong or shorten the interaction that we have with others as well as changing the quality of the interaction. (Unfortunately, if our behaviour is extreme the interaction is usually so short that we are unable to alter this initial impression.) We may indeed monitor the response of the other person and change our behaviour in the direction which appears to us to be congruent with the values of the other person. This awareness may not be present in the person with severe or profound learning difficulties, or at least not to the degree that leads to a planned altering of behaviour as a result of the reactions of others.

Adult-like behaviour is socially valued and sets up a quality of interaction that is marked by a certain amount of dignity and respect. There are important markers of this respect by the granting of certain 'privileges' which indicate the change in status. Thus, for example, adulthood is marked by the permission to marry, to vote, to drive a car, etc. These status symbols support the message that a person has reached the age where he or she is capable of making important decisions about their life. They usually go hand-in-hand with taking responsibility for oneself, forming longer-lasting relationships, economic self-sufficiency and independent living arrangements (Davies and Jenkins, 1994; FEU, 1991). Many of the adult markers are much less likely to be achieved by people with learning difficulties, yet it is essential that they are still given adult status with dignity and respect. It is with this in mind that we need to work towards encouraging age-appropriate behaviour.

It is worth reflecting on some of the ways in which people learn about appropriate and inappropriate behaviour in relation to changing age expectations. We must recognize that for the typically developing child there are powerful role models. Schools probably provide one of the most obvious sources because they are organized to differentiate between pupils on the basis of age. Differences between year groups are thereby strengthened. Older pupils may be perceived as having certain privileges. Typically during childhood there are also less subtle ways in which children are made aware of changing expectations. Adults for example may express certain rules – 'big boys don't cry', 'young ladies don't sit like that'. Both adults and peers also provide encouragement, support and reassurance about our styles and form of behaviour. Peer approval is often especially influential. Typically, therefore, children and young people are provided with models, rules, and with both direct and indirect feedback from parents, teachers and peers about the acceptability of behaviour.

It is not intended that this chapter should detail the socialization process for the typically developing child but to draw the readers attention to some important aspects which we need to consider in relation to pupils and young people with severe learning difficulties. First, we can see that adult-like behaviour emerges gradually. The transition from child-like to adult-like is not necessarily a smooth progression nor one that results in total change. It is, however, desirable to be able to discriminate at least at some level between occasions when child-like behaviour is perfectly acceptable and situations in which it is not. Second, and equally importantly, the reason for aspiring to adult-like behaviour is because of the respect and autonomy accorded to one. This is nicely demonstrated by Elwell (1993). She describes how she prepared for her daughter's stay in hospital by carefully selecting the clothes and toiletries her daughter took with her. As she says, 'I use baby powder, Nicola can't afford to' if others are going to interact with her in an age-appropriate way.

The development of age-appropriate behaviour can therefore be seen as an essential factor in ensuring that young people and adults with severe and profound learning difficulties engage in interaction in a manner that promotes dignity and respect. Although there are compelling reasons for fostering age-appropriate behaviour it is also recognized that there are a number of additional tensions which arise in relation to children and young people with SLD. These include first and foremost the likely disparate needs that arise from the developmental stage of the pupil in contrast to expectations based on physical maturity. It has been tempting in the past to reduce discussion of age-appropriate behaviour to consideration of developmental needs or chronological needs. This can now be seen to be an oversimplification of the issues. The development of age-appropriate behaviour is not an all-or-nothing phenomena but one that we can see in typically developing adolescents to be emergent but variable. It is important to remember this in establishing goals for pupils with severe and profound learning difficulties. Moreover, the readiness of pupils to assume more mature behaviour is likely to be individualized.

We must also consider the dilemmas that arise from fostering age-appropriate decision-making and choice where the outcome may be deemed by others to be age-inappropriate but the means to achieving it was adult-like. We may, for example, encourage pupils to make their own choices and decisions but be faced with a quandary when we see the choice they have made. Such dilemmas rightly make us consider both the ends and the means of our teaching. They may also make us ask ourselves exactly what the choice was in this situation (Coupe O'Kane *et al.*, 1994). Finally, we must reflect on the relationship between parental and school aspirations and to consider fully the rationales on which these are based, again taking into account cultural issues as well as age.

In the following sections we aim to highlight some of the central practical issues for schools (and other institutions) to consider in relation to developing a sense of progression in establishing age-appropriate behaviours.

Staff Behaviour

This seems a good place to start as we have recognized in the beginning the two-way nature of the process. It is often unwittingly that staff interact with pupils in a way that promotes immaturity and sometimes even dependent behaviour. It must be recognized that such responses may serve to reduce conflict within ourselves. It may, for example, make behaviour easier to accept or understand; it may usefully bring about a natural response of protecting and nurturing. Once styles of interaction are established they are very difficult to change as there is security for both partners in a predictable exchange. It is important, however, for staff to fully consider whether their style of interaction (and by this we include all teaching interaction as well as informal casual interaction) is impeding progression or fostering it. For example, with pupils/students whose

62

communicative responses are very limited, we may find ourselves adopting styles that we naturally use with very young children, exaggerating intonation, using closed questions and using a high register (e.g., who-o-ose eaten all their dinner?). This is a difficult response to override as these interactional features are clearly effective in gaining the attention of pupils functioning at an early stage of development – but perhaps we could explore different ways of securing attention and maximizing understanding. Equally we might find ourselves responding positively to the pupil who rushes up to us for a hug. If we stop and asks ourself what we would do if the person was at least as tall as us, then the reasonableness of our behaviour can be questioned. We may be utilizing the same terms of endearment that we used when the pupil/student was much younger. If inadvertently we are fostering the behaviour and outlook of a young child, how can we expect the pupil/student to develop maturity?

The difficulty that some parents have with accepting the changing status of their son or daughter is well documented (Baker, 1991; Walsh *et al.*, 1988). In some instances this lack of acceptance can serve to create tension between home and school and call for the utmost diplomacy and sensitivity on the part of teachers. In the introduction we pointed to the progressive nature of the transition to adulthood; if the school has an explicit policy which supports this process, parents can alter their expectations over time.

The Curriculum

Historically we have adopted a curriculum which is based on a hierarchical structure, often stages, with an in-built notion of ascending the ladder, one rung at a time. The model for this has been typical child development, thus focusing teachers' attention on the behaviours of young typically developing children. Alongside this developmentally-driven curriculum has been a functional curriculum which has largely derived its content and rationale from analysis of the daily demands on adults. These two frameworks are not inherently incompatible but have often led to quite contrasting contexts for teaching, the one based on activities of the typical young child and the other based on the supposed skills of independent adults. In these circumstances it is perhaps unsurprising that teachers were sometimes struggling to keep an appropriate perspective on the needs of young people who are neither young children nor adults. One might argue that the National Curriculum has the inherent advantage that it forces a move away from a developmental curriculum and encourages more age-appropriate contexts for developing knowledge, skills and understanding. A number of different approaches to the National Curriculum are currently being discussed (Coupe O'Kane *et al.*, 1994; Frew and Emblem, 1994; Humphreys, 1994; Ware, 1994) it is hoped that whatever approach individual schools choose, there is as full consideration of contexts for learning as there is of content.

Pupil behaviour

It is interesting to consider which pupil behaviour we consider child-like and which causes us concern. A recent small-scale survey we carried out in school suggested that there was considerable variation amongst members of staff in the behaviours they considered to be chronologically inappropriate. For example, crying when one couldn't get one's own way, singing a goodbye song when you are a teenager, looking at picture books (Dick Bruna) when one is a teenager, playing a musical box. This raised a number of questions for the researchers. Is it because of the contrast between the pupil's physical maturity and the behaviour? Does the behaviour itself offend? Is it because we think (or indeed know) that the pupil is capable of more complex behaviours? Is it because the behaviour is one that has continued without changing for such a long period of time (years possibly)? Is it because the pupil/student does not differentiate between contexts? Questions of this kind enable us to be clearer about differences between our own perspectives on the behaviour, and the perspective of the pupil. This helps us to be more sensitive to the needs and feelings of the pupil in planning for change and to be aware of the ways in which our own 'prejudices' may be biasing our viewpoint.

Institutional Practices

In the introduction we highlighted the importance of 'markers' that served to reinforce the idea of advancing age and how the organization and ethos of the school serves to differentiate between pupils on the basis of age. In contrast, special schools can obfuscate such differences. They may not organize classes on the basis of age and consequently be attempting to provide an appropriate environment for both 3- and 13-year-olds. Equally, again unlike the majority of mainstream schools, they may name classes in a non-hierarchical way, after groups of objects, colours, or animals. These practices serve to reduce expectations rather than highlight important age differences. We cannot hope to delineate the gradual changes from childhood to adulthood if we cannot even recognize extreme differences of need.

If the organization does not serve to draw attention to advancing age and if pupils are not grouped by chronological age, then it is hard to provide an environment which reflects this diversity. In these circumstances it is likely that provision is dictated by the needs of the younger pupils, a situation that will be exacerbated by the scarcity of resources for the older pupils.

It is important to also question whole-school practices where meeting the needs of one group of pupils may run counter to meeting those of another. It is entirely appropriate for the nursery class to be enjoying singing 'The wheels on the bus' in their class, but it becomes much harder to justify when this activity is transposed into one for whole-school assemblies.

Creating Change

Bearing in mind our initial reflections, it is important that any programme for change

- recognizes the interactive nature of staff and pupil behaviour,
- remembers that such change may well be gradual,
- recognizes that there are contextual issues, and
- that a polar position is likely to be unreasonable.

With these aspects in mind, we start by recommending that an audit of the schools management of the transition to adulthood is undertaken.

School Audit

We have drawn inspiration for this audit from Galloway and Banes (1994) to assess how pupils' educational experiences change as they move from nursery to school-leaving age. It is not intended as a blueprint but as a useful starting place which will involve all school staff and which might reasonably serve to inform a policy document.

1. Curriculum

Schools could start by specifying the ways in which the curricular areas differ for pupils through the key stages. (i.e., nursery, KS1, KS2, KS3, KS4, 16–19). When does the school introduce curricula such as sex education, family life, independent travel, use of leisure time, citizenship, gender and race issues, advocacy? Is there a sense of progression to the presentation, teaching approach and expected outcomes for areas and topics which span the years? If a topic approach is used within school, then again it is important to audit how the approach and content varies between age groups. More widely, the school needs to examine how the programmes of study change with key stages independent of the level of attainment.

2. Resources
The main resources in the school can be assessed for the appropriateness of their content and design to pupils of different ages. These might include: libraries (fiction, non-fiction, magazines and comics), leisure equipment (for use both outside and inside), videos and films, computer programs, multicultural resources, music and songs, posters, curriculum-related materials, etc.

The environment also constitutes an important resource in addition to contributing to the ethos of the school. Again, one might audit the extent to which it differentiates between the needs of younger and older pupils. Included within the environmental resources would be display material (both 'home-made' and commercial), mobiles, the type of furnishing and its arrangement.

3. Whole-school activities
Within this one might include a comprehensive review of activities that involve the whole school (such as assemblies, sports days, concerts, outings, etc.) and those activities which are routines adopted by the whole school (such as the use of registers, and lunch-time arrangements). The emphasis on this activity is to ask how the experiences are differentiated for pupils of different ages. It is easy to assume that because activities occur in separate groups they do in fact follow a different format. Included in common routines are care routines and the extent to which gender is taken into account.

4. Relationship between staff and students
From the point of pupil participation, it is important to examine the extent to which pupils/students of different ages take an active part in the learning process. This might, for example, focus on the extent to which pupils make 'real' choices, evaluate their own progress, take part in reviews and multidisciplinary meetings, share in the decision-making processes of the school, etc.

From the point of view of staff interactions, it is not only the extent to which they empower individuals to contribute to the aforementioned activities but the extent to which they communicate more subtly their awareness and expectations as pupils get older. For example, the tone of voice, vocabulary used, the type of physical contact they have, the way in which they address individuals, the involvement in discussion when a

66

third person is present, all serve to communicate the way in which a person is viewed and should reflect a changing status as the pupil moves through childhood into adulthood.

Individual Intervention

It is likely that the school audit will lead to development in policies and changes in action. It may, however, still be necessary to supplement the outcome of the audit with plans for individual intervention. We include two cases studies as an example of how one school has approached forming an individual programme. Again these are not intended to form blueprints but to highlight how a confident philosophy can inform practice by providing clear guidance in the decision-making processes.

The starting place for both case studies was to consider the "behaviour of concern" both from the perspective of the person themselves and of others. This ensures that the analysis of why the 'behaviour is causing concern' and the options for intervention address the needs of the individual.

Case Study 1 – Sarah

The first case study is of a 13-year-old girl who attends an all-age SLD school. The staff have expressed concern that she 'constantly' approaches adults with a request to sing, 'Wind the bobbin up'. If we start by thinking about the function or meaning of this behaviour for Sarah, we can quickly see that this request usually leads to a joint interaction that is predictable and pleasurable.

From a language perspective we can see this action as regulating joint attention. From the staff perspective this behaviour is seen as 'attention seeking' and inappropriate given her age and the fact that she is able to speak in two- to four-word phrases and is therefore potentially capable of other forms of spoken interaction. A number of possible options for intervention were initially considered– teaching her alternative songs, ignoring her requests, or limiting the number of times staff would sing this song. In a sense all of these options were pursued but not before staff had looked in more detail at the opportunities for interaction and the type of conversation she enjoyed with others. It quickly became apparent that her attempts to engage others in conversation were limited. Equally, staff found it difficult to engage her in conversation. In locating the area of need we were able to shift the focus of intervention to creating opportunities for interaction with both peers and adults where their was a common framework. This was provided through 'conversation' books: scrap books that were compiled by both pupils and staff that were based around particular areas of interest – trips out, television programmes, sport (Musselwhite, 1990). In this way both the pupil, peers and staff were provided with topics in which to share attention. In order to ensure that these books did not became as routine (or repetitive) as 'Wind the bobbin up', care was taken to develop the contexts in which they were used, for example by using them with different peers. A second aspect to the intervention was to examine the role of singing and music within the class and to teach new songs. A symbol board was kept to reveal the choice of songs sung in the week with an emphasis on 'new songs' and a class rule negotiated that 'old songs' could only be included once per week but that this would be reviewed. At assembly the class sung some of their 'new songs' so that other staff were aware of the changing repertoire.

Case Study 2 – Phillip

Our second case study concerns Phillip, a young man of 17 years who has profound learning difficulties and is described by staff as having 'autistic tendencies' in that he is rather withdrawn, although he does not reject social interaction. In contrast to Sarah, he does not yet communicate intentionally although he does express his likes and dislikes. In many ways this case study reveals a number of the additional tensions that surround intervention with a pupil who have a fairly limited number of interests and responses.

The 'behaviour of concern' for staff here is the attachment to a music box produced by a well-known manufacturer of toys for small children. Phillip listens to this box whenever he can and will seek the box out if it is not immediately available, showing great signs of distress when it is taken from him. Once again, we look at the perspective of the person and the staff. Clearly Phillip enjoys the music and holding the box. Although we cannot be sure, it appears that having the box provides some measure of security. The staff feel that whilst it is ok to have the box at some times, it should not be something which accompanies him everywhere and is used to avoid engaging in other activities. Clearly a number of options exist – some of which have already been tried, for example, substituting the sound and/or visual appearance, limiting opportunities to have the box, using it to encourage the development of new skills, etc. Whilst the staff were concerned to change the behaviour, they were also committed to ensuring that any strategies did not cause Phillip distress. This suggested that any direct intervention had to be planned for very slow change over a considerable time span. Given Phillip's attachment to this object, it was decided to utilize the box to encourage the development of new skills, initially by showing Phillip that it was placed inside other containers which required

68

unfastening, and teaching him to 'find' it. Teaching would provide careful 'scaffolding' of help to ensure that Phillip was not distressed by this activity. Over time, Phillip would spend longer on gaining access to this box. To supplement this teaching programme, staff would explore and develop Phillip's liking for other music. It is hoped that this combined approach will lead to a decrease in the desirability of the box through the increasing effort involved to access it, and that other music will increase in desirability and perhaps start to replace it. A third aspect was that Phillip would be encouraged to have the box nearby but not to hold it, with the aim over time of gradually moving the box further away. Like the previous case study, the process of intervention is slow but steady.

As you will see, both case study programmes are developed following full consideration of the nature of the behaviour, its possible function for the individual pupil, and the extent to which change can and should be planned for. As with any teaching programme, they are based on an assessment of need and a plan that incorporates a clear sense of progression with gradual change towards age-appropriate behaviour.

Conclusion

This chapter has been written with a view to helping the reader to explore some of the issues and dilemmas encountered in promoting a policy of age-appropriate behaviour. Whilst we have not aimed to set out a formula for achieving this, we have included examples which we hope will be helpful in aiding schools (and other institutions) to adopt an approach which strives to ensure that in the wider context, young people achieve a status which gives them the dignity and respect accorded to other adults.

References

Baker, P.A. (1991) 'The denial of adolescence for people with mental handicaps: An unwitting conspiracy?', *Mental Handicap*, 19, 2, 61–5.
Coupe O'Kane, J., Porter J. and Taylor A. (1994), 'Meaningful content and contexts for learning', in Coupe O'Kane, J. and Smith, B. (Eds) *Taking Control: Enabling people with learning difficulties*, London: David Fulton.
Davies, C. and Jenkins, R. (1994) 'Negotiating adult status: how people with learning difficulties are disadvantaged', *Down's Syndrome Association Newsletter*, No 73.
Elwell, L. (1993) 'Age appropriateness', *Information Exchange*, 37, 8–9.
Further Education Unit (1991) *Adult Status for All?*, London: FEU.
Frew, B., and Emblem, B. (1994) 'A modular curriculum', *The SLD Experience*, 9, 14–16.

Galloway, S. and Banes, R. (1994) 'Beyond the simple audit', in Rose, R., Fergusson, A., Coles, C., Byers, R. and Banes, R. *Implementing the Whole Curriculum for Pupils with Learning Difficulties*, London: David Fulton.

Humphreys, K. (1994) 'An irrational curriculum', *The SLD Experience*, 9,1.

Matson, J.L. Sadowski, C., Matese, M. and Benavidez, D. (1993) 'Empirical study of mental health professionals' knowledge and attitudes towards the concept of age appropriateness', *Mental Retardation*, 31, 5, 340–45.

Musselwhite, C. (1990) 'Topic setting: Generic and specific strategies', paper presented at the 4th biennial ISAAC Conference, Stockholm, 13–16 August.

Taylor, P. (1993) 'For ages nothing happened', *Information Exchange*, 38, 4–6.

Walsh, P., Coyle, K., and Lynch, C. (1988) 'The Partners Project. Community-based recreation for adults with mental handicaps', *Mental Handicap*, 16, 122–5.

Ware, J. (1994) 'Implementing the 1988 Act with pupils with PMLD', in Ware, J. (ed.) *Educating Children with Profound and Multiple Learning Difficulties*, London: David Fulton.

CHAPTER 6

Discussion: Age-appropriate or Developmentally-appropriate Activities?

Beryl Smith

It is difficult to produce a balanced commentary on the two previous chapters because I am sitting, very precariously, on the fence between the two. I agree with both points of view! The writers have been courageous to espouse their viewpoints, as feelings on the subject often run high. They have succeeded in opening up the debate by presenting different, but not necessarily opposing views. They have not adopted extreme positions but acknowledge that the central issue is meeting the various and varied needs of people with learning disability.

When discussing the definition of appropriate behaviour, Jill Porter, Nicola Grove and Keith Park acknowledge that, even when reaching or having reached maturity, we do not uniformly adopt so-called 'adult-like' behaviours. Many, maybe the majority of us, indulge in 'child-like' behaviour at times, associated with expression of emotions such as pleasure or anger or frustration. However, we generally regulate out behaviour according to the situation because we recognize the link between what we do and the way others treat us. If we display 'adult-like' behaviour we are accorded a certain amount of dignity and respect and the privileges which go with adult status. They consider that people with severe learning difficulties should be helped to recognize the reasons for aspiring to adult-like behaviour, helped to attain it but also to have some understanding of when child-like behaviours are acceptable and when they are not. They discuss ways in which educators may foster development of adult-like behaviour as the child grows older by means of age-appropriate progression in curriculum, resources, activities and staff: student relationships but are also well aware of the needs relating to developmental stage, stating that 'a polar position is likely to be unreasonable'. Surely no one argues with that?

Melanie Nind and Dave Hewett aim to facilitate the social and communication development of people with severe and complex learning disability and challenging behaviour by means of an approach based on the kind of experiences found in care-giver-infant interaction. Having received objections from some practitioners regarding lack of 'age-appropriateness', they examined their practice in the context of normalization or social role valorization. They present persuasive arguments that they are indeed paying respect to clients by attempting to meet their most demanding needs, that offering experiences appropriate to a client's chronological age will not bring about adult-like behaviour if those experiences are beyond his or her comprehension, and also that 'helping to make people with learning difficulties more acceptable' by means of age-appropriate experiences, places the onus for acceptance on their shoulders, rather than on society. Nind and Hewett point out that people likely to benefit from their approach are often unable to relate to others and are those for whom other approaches have failed. Surely no one argues with that?

The writers are concerned with the same aim, if they will allow me to simplify their arguments – that of optimizing the chances for people with learning disability to live as satisfying and fulfilled lives as possible. They are emphasizing, for the purpose of debate, different ways in which this aim might be achieved, for people of different ages, at different levels of development. Any approaches which are advocated as facilitating the worth and well-being of people with learning disability are worth serious consideration and a difference of opinion as to which is the more important is worth pursuing. Division between the two approaches is most obvious and most debated in relation to adults with learning disability, since 'normal' or age-appropriate behaviour and living style has to a large extent become synonymous with community care and acceptance by 'society'.

The concept of normalization, (discussed by Nind and Hewett), seen as a basis for current service development, has been defined in various ways by different people. The present pervasive influence is that of Wolfensberger, who is concerned with the way in which deviance can be produced and also transmuted. To counteract the perceived deviance of people with learning disability, he advocates the use of culturally valued means to enable them to lead valued lives in living conditions at least as good as those of the average citizen, enhancement of their behaviour, appearance, experience and status and the use of culturally normative means to support behaviour, appearance, experience and status (Wolfensberger, 1980). He stresses (Wolfensberger, 1992) that services for people with learning disability need to address both the enhancement of their competences and of their social image in order that they are given acceptance, respect and autonomy and can lead almost totally integrated, highly valued, productive and full lives. While the normalization principle has proved popular with service providers in their attempt to improve the care and quality of life of people with learning disability, it is not without its critics. Chappell (1992) suggests that in offering a theory of how to improve services, it has allowed service providers to adapt to deinstutionalization and at the same time to retain their key role in the lives of people with learning disability. She points out the danger of allowing the definition of quality of care and quality of life for people with learning disability to be dominated by the normalization principle rather than the views of service users.

Problems arise when we, the so-called 'normal' population, start to define what is required for people with learning disability to live satisfying and fulfilled lives. We may assume that one particular theory or aspect of a theory is the most important or even the only possible pathway towards such a life. Some consider that personal development is very important, as is acceptance by 'society', achieved by living a similar lifestyle to one's peers and participating in a similar range of activities. Others focus on rights and responsibilities and opportunities to make choices. Judgements about which of these aspects is the most important are not productive. However, what may be helpful is acknowledgement that adoption of a particular stance may be influenced by our own difficulties and inadequacies in meeting the range of very varied needs of people with learning disability. It is easier to concentrate on the practical implications of one aspect of a theory than to encompass the many and diverse experiences, opportunities and resources which human beings require to fulfil themselves, and which afford each person 'acceptance, respect and autonomy' (Wolfensberger, 1992).

Among members of the general population, both age-appropriate and, on occasion, non-age-appropriate activities are considered to be acceptable. We also engage in a wide range of activities, many of which are not developmentally-appropriate if we define that term as behaviour suited to our most advanced level of intellectual development. If we assume that most of us, as members of the general population, are striving for fulfilled and satisfying lives, even if we do not always attain them, this mixture of activities and experiences, and freedom to choose the proportions of the mixture, are what constitute what we think of as a 'normal' life. We may, if we wish, balance the demands of a cerebral job by playing with a train set in the evening, kicking a ball around the garden, playing snap, cleaning the kitchen sink or even sitting staring into space. Some of these activities are not age-appropriate and probably none are developmentally-appropriate. Having a range of activities available to us and decision-making skills which enable us to exercise control over aspects of our life is probably more important to the majority of people than being considered 'normal'. It may be that the situation is similar for people with learning disability. But at this point it could be useful to consider evidence for the importance of age-appropriate and developmentally-appropriate activities in helping people with learning disability to receive acceptance, respect and autonomy.

Matson *et al.* (1993) point out that attitudes and beliefs on the subject of age-appropriateness are currently poorly supported by research. They surveyed the views of mental health professionals (administrators, professionals and paraprofessionals). While around two thirds of respondents felt that age-appropriateness is always important for people with severe learning disability, there was an interesting difference between respondents according to occupation. Professionals were far more likely than administrators and paraprofessionals to say that other factors, in addition to age-appropriateness, should be considered in treatment programmes. It is tempting to speculate (which the authors did not) that administrators and paraprofessionals may elevate the status of age-appropriate experiences because of their link to ideas of acceptance, respect and autonomy. Loosely defined and applied, age-appropriateness is an easily implemented aspect of life for people with severe learning disability. As Nind and Hewett point out, insistence on age-appropriate behaviour may also disguise a fear on the part of practitioners that clients will cause them embarrassment in public. Professionals, with their presumably greater knowledge of the intricacies of learning and development, might be more prepared to take other factors into account in treatment programmes.

The relationship between various 'age-appropriate' practices and outcome in terms of social acceptance and respect, although largely credited as positive, has also not been verified empirically. In an investigation of the effect of age-appropriate activities on adults' perception of a person with learning difficulties, Calhoun and Calhoun (1993) videotaped a young woman with Down's Syndrome in two situations. In one she participated in leisure activities considered by the researchers to be typical for young women (reading a *National Geographic* magazine, playing a card game, and clipping grocery store coupons from the newspaper). In the other, she participated in leisure activities designed for much younger persons (reading a children's book, playing a children's board game). Undergraduate university students were randomly assigned to one of the two viewing conditions and asked, among other questions, about whether or not they liked the person depicted in the video and their willingness to interact with her. There were no significant differences in ratings of the two groups, although views were generally positive. Caution must be displayed in interpreting the implications of this experiment, since the participants were not representative of the general population and the effect of their perceptions on their behaviour is not known. The findings are useful, however, in that they should make us aware that social acceptance may not be enhanced by requiring people with learning difficulties to engage in what are considered to be age-appropriate activities. One wonders if reading a *National Geographic* magazine was an enjoyable and meaningful occupation for a young woman with Down's Syndrome. Observers may have been aware of the probable surface nature of the activity, of the 'cloak of competence' which it afforded. Perhaps people prefer, if they have a choice, to interact with people with learning difficulty who are motivated to participate in a particular activity, whether or not it is entirely age-appropriate.

An additional problem in the debate is that although the concept of age-appropriateness is considered to be aimed at eliciting acceptance and respect for individuals with learning disability (Nirje, 1969), decisions on the way in which it is to be implemented lie in the minds of people who live and work with people with learning disability – parents, teachers, social workers, care assistants, nurses, day centre staff, etc. When 'we' choose what we consider to be age-appropriate experiences, are we not in danger of choosing something inappropriate, shaped by our own experiences and attitudes? Jill Porter and colleagues discuss the value of age-appropriate curriculum, resources, activities and relationships for children and young people but also mention the tension which may develop between home and school if parents object to their son or daughter participating in activities pursued by their age peers. It may be that parents' objections stem from a misplaced wish to protect their son or daughter from the dangers of the adult world. This is likely, given the circumstances, but it may also be a reflection of parents' ideas on what they consider to be age-appropriate behaviour. Some older mothers and fathers used to (and some from my observation still do), encourage their son with learning disability to dress in a suit with a tie, even when going out to the high street to shop, because that is what is 'proper' for a grown up man and would afford them more respect than being dressed in jeans. Daughters might be afforded more respect if they are dressed modestly (like mother) and don't go out at night to discos. Parents' motivation is similar to that of formal carers who also encourage adults with learning disability to engage in what they consider to be normal behaviour. It may mean sitting down in the evening to look at the television, having trendy clothes, going down to the pub or for a ride in a car (minibus), or going abroad for a holiday. The reasoning is that if people with learning disability do what other people do and look like other people, they will receive acceptance and respect. Whether or not these examples of age-appropriate behaviour do afford individuals acceptance and respect is not really clear, neither is it clear whether they encourage autonomy, defined as 'personal freedom', 'freedom of the will' (*Concise Oxford Dictionary*). However, if asked, carers produce 'evidence' that these experiences are 'good' for the individual – they thoroughly enjoyed the trip, they are tired after spending the day at the day centre and like to sit down to look at the television, and so on.

The above studies and comments relate to adults with learning disability and while they indicate that age-appropriate activities are not likely to present a short cut to acceptance and respect and autonomy, most people would agree intuitively with Jill Porter and her colleagues when they write that age-appropriate behaviour is likely to facilitate interaction and furthermore 'set up a quality of interaction which is marked by a certain amount of dignity and respect'. Individuals may also develop more functional skills when in situations in which expectations and opportunities are age-appropriate. However, given the wide variation in needs among the population of people with learning difficulties, there is not likely to be a stock of activities which is of benefit to all. A person with learning difficulties who wears designer jeans, who goes shopping in Sainsburys, accompanied by care assistants, is probably not going to get very much from the experience or be more valued if she has little understanding of the meaning of the situation and has no means of interacting with people around. Might she not stand a better chance of developing functional skills, of being valued and also of enjoying herself, if someone used that time to imitate the noises she makes and encourage, her to initiate interactions and signal choices?

Similar questions need to be asked about evidence for the value for the person with learning disability of developmentally-appropriate activities. Does provision of activities matched to the level of a person's cognitive understanding facilitate personal and social development and thereby the opportunity to achieve respect, value and autonomy?

Nind and Hewett refer to the educational implications of Piagetian theory of cognitive development, which is essentially that understanding is constructed from within the individual by means of exploration and interaction with both the social environment and the material environment of objects and events. The emergence of developmentally more advanced behaviours is considered to result from knowledge obtained by exploring and being helped to explore the environment, by practising current behaviours and experimenting in their wider use. The concept of stages of development, during which the individual displays particular types of mental structures for dealing with information, is of importance in that stage-appropriate or developmentally-appropriate activities are considered to facilitate reorganization of thinking which leads to the formation of more advanced mental structures. By stage-appropriate is meant those activities which offer some challenge and interest to the individual but do not pose unmanageable difficulties, or on the other hand are not too easy and therefore of little interest or value for further cognitive development. The essential characteristic of developmentally-appropriate activities is that the individual is actively engaged with his or her environment and that they offer the opportunity for progression in understanding.

Other theorists have also explored the concept of activities and experiences which are appropriate to various stages in cognitive development. Vygotsky (1978) draws attention to the role of the adult. His theory is that mental development proceeds through a series of stages which are characterized by the amount of help required from the 'expert' adult, or cognitively more advanced peer, who provides assistance until no longer needed by the novice learner. The process of providing graduated assistance has been termed 'scaffolding', since a scaffold is a temporary and adjustable support which can be removed when no longer necessary (Bruner and Connolly, 1974). Being on hand to help, to model, to encourage, but not to take over, has been observed to be an effective strategy in interactions between adults and children which aim to promote cognitive development (Wood *et al.*, 1976). It is from these theories of intellectual development that the practice stems of providing people with learning disability with activities which are developmentally-appropriate. Suitable activities may not be those engaged in by the majority of people of the same age but efforts are usually made in the case of adults to employ materials which are age-appropriate in order to avoid stigmatization.

For young children with learning disability, there is generally no problem in applying an approach which advocates developmentally-appropriate activities since it does not conflict with age-appropriateness. The most appropriate and helpful interventions in infancy and early childhood are those which establish a satisfying relationship with care-givers which, in turn, leads to increased stimulation, attention and support (Calhoun and Rose, 1988). Because infants with severe learning disability are likely to be less responsive to social stimulation and less ready to explore their environment, attention is paid to enhancing the opportunities for interaction and exploration and thus, the opportunity for cognitive development.

There is a danger, however, of expecting that provision of developmentally-appropriate activities will automatically lead to opportunities for interaction and onwards to further cognitive development. Findings from a study which examined the relationship of quality of mother:child interactions to developmental functioning of children with learning disability, highlighted the importance of developing the child's feeling of competence, esteem and motivation to engage in further exploration, rather than requiring engagement in certain activities (Mahoney et al., 1985). Responsiveness to children's feeling and interests, responsiveness to activities which they themselves initiate, cooperation and enjoyment were all characteristics associated with interactions experienced by children at the highest level of developmental functioning. Interactions experienced by children at the lowest levels were classified as 'directive and teaching orientated'. An objection to these findings is that the quality of interactions might vary according to whether or not the child was making progress in development; lack of development might elicit a 'directive and teaching orientated' style. However, a further study (Mahoney and Powell, 1988) of the results of an intervention programme for young children with learning disability found the rate of developmental change to be significantly associated with parental style of interaction but not with the children's level of developmental functioning at the start of the programme.

In a summary of results of early intervention programmes, Mahoney and Robinson (1992) say that they 'provide additional support for the tenets of developmentally appropriate practices' but make the point that the most effective style of interaction is one which accepts and values the behaviours that children are able to do, is highly responsive to their interests, and provides them with the opportunity to exercise control over the activities in which they are involved. As with the provision of age-appropriate activities, developmentally-appropriate activities, of themselves, probably do not afford individuals a short cut to acceptance, respect and autonomy. What they can do is to foster motivation, a sense of control and self-esteem.

Programmes in schools for children with learning difficulties went through a period in which a 'directive and teaching orientated' style was paramount in an effort to produce proficiency in skills aimed at maximum autonomy. Teachers are now generally far more aware of the benefits of an interactive teaching style: one which involves the child and young person in their own learning. Skills, knowledge and understanding underlying autonomy develop in contexts which are enjoyable, motivating and which offer choice (Coupe O'Kane et al., 1994). Byers (1994) also makes the point that autonomy is more than proficiency in skills and says that the issue is not concerned with the ability of teachers to devise sophisticated sets of skills but with 'whether teachers have the courage to support their pupils in taking increasing responsibility for their learning' – and ultimately to take control of their lives. This same issue of power relationships is apparent in adult services in which, although the objectives of professionals and clients may be similar, the manner in which they are to be attained is different. Oliver (1989) gives the example of professionals for whom independence refers to self-care activities, such as washing and dressing, and clients for whom the same objective refers to autonomy and being able to control one's life.

Could it be that in order to enable children and adults with learning disability to achieve a happy and fulfilled life, or in Wolfensberger's words, to aspire to totally integrated, highly valued, productive and full lives (assuming that is their goal also), that we are in danger of not seeing the wood for the trees? Perhaps we should pay less attention to what is age-appropriate or developmentally-appropriate and concentrate on the process by means of which each person is enabled to interact with his or her environment, to control aspects of that environment, and above all to experience the satisfaction, self-esteem and stimulus to further development which comes with such achievements. Age-appropriate activities and developmentally-appropriate activities are not prescriptions, but can be means to that end. Both indicate respect for the person and concern for their dignity, because both have the aim of furthering that person's well-being. But the balance between the two is likely to be different for different people.

We need to look at the range of ways in which positive regard for people with learning difficulties can be established. The acceptance and respect of society is accorded for different reasons. Money, material possessions and fashionable clothes are one recipe for acceptance; behaviour which conforms to current social norms is also of importance (despite the fact that it varies for different age groups, different strata of society and different sexes). Competence in one's job, one's daily living and personal relationships also brings acceptance and respect. However, positive regard depends on something more complex than competence, external acquisitions and acceptable behaviour; an essential component is our own self–regard. Placing emphasis on the need for people with learning difficulties to develop skills and/or acceptable behaviour is something which professionals tend to do in order to fit them into the services provided (Cattermole et al., 1990). In their research on the quality of life for people with learning difficulties who moved to community homes, these writers consulted the service users. Service users wanted better social lives, more freedom and choice. They gave low priority to the learning of skills relative to these other aspirations. They preferred staff who gave adequate help, advice and other forms of support but were not unduly restrictive, to those seen as either authoritarian or distant. These favoured 'quality of life' characteristics recall the characteristics of successful intervention programmes discussed above.

Perhaps the key aspect of promoting a satisfying and fulfilled life for a person with learning disability is helping that person to develop motivation, self-esteem and a sense of control, by encouraging and supporting interests and maximizing opportunities for success. We function 'normally' when we experiment, develop skills, make relationships and enjoy ourselves. None of us achieves this to perfection, but value and autonomy come with the extent to which we can participate in these processes. While age-appropriateness and developmental-appropriateness are both important concerns, maybe we should concentrate more on what is 'person-appropriate'.

References

Bruner, J. and Connolly, K. (1974) *The Growth of Competence*, London: Academic Press.
Byers, R. (1994) 'Teaching as dialogue: teaching approaches and learning styles in schools for pupils with learning difficulties', in Coupe O'Kane J. and Smith, B. (eds) *Taking Control: Enabling people with learning difficulties*, London: David Fulton.
Calhoun, M-L. and Calhoun, G. (1993) 'Age-appropriate activities: effects on the social perception of adults with mental retardation', *Education and Training in Mental Retardation*, 28, 143–8.
Calhoun, M. and Rose, T. (1988) 'Early social reciprocity interventions for infants with severe retardation: current findings and implications for the future', *Education and Training in Mental Retardation*, 23, 340–3
Cattermole, M., Jahoda, A. and Markova, I. (1990) 'Quality of life for people with learning difficulties moving to community homes', *Disability, Handicap and Society*, 5, 137–152
Chappell, A. (1992) 'Towards as sociological critique of the normalisation principle', *Disability, Handicap and Society*, 7, 35–51
Coupe O'Kane, J., Porter, J. and Taylor, A. (1994) 'Meaningful content and context for learning', in Coupe O'Kane, J. and Smith, B. (eds) *Taking Control: Enabling people with learning difficulties*, London: David Fulton
Mahoney,G., Finger, I. and Powell, A. (1985) 'Relationship of maternal behavioral style to the development of handicapped children', *American Journal of Mental Deficiency*, 90, 298–302.
Mahoney, G. and Powell, A. (1988) 'Modifying parent–child interaction: enhancing the development of handicapped children', *Journal of Special Education*, 22, 82–96.

Mahoney, G. and Robinson, C. (1992) 'Focusing on parent-child interaction: The bridge to developmentally appropriate practices', *Topics in Early Childhood Special Education*, 12, 105–120.

Matson, J., Sadowski, C., Matese, M. and Benavidez, D. (1993) 'Empirical study of mental health professionals' knowledge and attitudes towards the concept of age appropriateness', *Mental Retardation*, 31, 340–5.

Nirje, B. (1969) 'The normalization principle and its human management implications', in Kugel, R. and Wolfensberger, W. (eds) *Changing Patterns of Residential Services for the Mentally Retarded*, Washington, DC: President's Committee on Mental Retardation.

Oliver, M. (1989) 'Disability and dependency: a creation of industrial societies?', in Barton, L. (ed.) *Disability and Dependency*, London: Falmer Press.

Vygotsky, L.S. (1978) *Mind in Society*, Cambridge, Mass: Harvard University Press.

Wolfensberger, W. (1980) 'A brief overview of the principle of normalization', in Flynn, R. and Nitsh, K. (eds) *Normalization, Social Integration and Community Services*, Baltimore, MD: University Park Press.

Wolfensberger, W. (1992) *A Brief Introduction to Social Role Valorization as a Higher Order Concept for Structuring Human Services* (2nd revised edn), Syracuse, NY: Training Institute for Human Service Planning, Leadership and Change Agency.

Wood, D. (1989) 'Social interaction as tutoring', in Bornstein, B. and Bruner, J. (eds), *Crosscurrents in Contemporary Psychology*, Hillsdale, NJ: LEA.

Wood, D, Bruner, J. and Ross, G. (1976) 'The role of training in problem solving', *Journal of Child Psychology and Psychiatry*, 17, 89–100.

Part 3
Integration for Whom?

CHAPTER 7

Integration, Inclusion – What does it all mean?

John Hall

Is Segregation Better for Some Children?

This chapter is not for the academics who, before reading even this far, will already have flipped through to the end to scan the reference list and check out the author's paradigm. They will be disappointed to find few if any references on inclusion and none at all relating to research on integration. The reader will not find those satisfying (to some) little references that serve to reassure the uncertain that they are indeed hearing the voice of the 'expert' who knows his or her stuff because he or she has read everyone else's.

'Integration' and 'inclusion' are not subjects, they are notions or concepts and, just occasionally, they are banners on the street. Not only is the author not an expert on the integration of children with special needs, he does not even believe such people exist. There are people who take a firm stand for or against special schools; people who research important variables related to integrated or segregated schooling; people who are paid to work with children in ordinary or segregated settings; there are psychologists and advisers who sport the title of 'expert' on the needs of children; and there are inspectors who assess the quality of educational experience offered to children in diverse settings in order to pronounce upon its value. Some of these people will have first-hand knowledge of what does or does not work for children in this or that setting, while others will have only anecdotal knowledge of these things. All, though, will have their own position on 'integration' and a personal view on how things should be ordered. Many also will have a firm view about 'inclusion', having attended a conference or two over the past five years and read the odd book or article on the subject.

Nevertheless, there are as yet no experts on the matter because we have no agreement on what the matter is. The issue of integrated vs segregated education is simply too complex with far too many disparate paradigms and perspectives to be approached in the simplistic way it so often is – as though there could be an answer to a question that begs so many further questions.

The model of need used throughout this chapter is that of a child with severe and/or complex needs such that he or she would typically receive their education in a school for pupils with severe learning difficulties (SLD). The focus is restricted in this way because it is impossibly difficult to generalize about children with special educational needs who may be said to constitute 20 per cent of the school population.

In what follows, the simple assumption will be made that we cannot know the answer to the question, 'Do some children learn better in integrated or segregated settings?' This is not to say that it does not have the form and intent required for a question to have meaning, but rather that it contains too many unexplicated assumptions. Hence it is reasonable to ask just what is meant by learn better, integrated, and segregated.

Making sense of 'assumptions'

To ask whether a child learns better in one setting than another begs the question of which aspects of learning are seen to be important. In strictly curricula terms it may be assumed that a child with SLD has needs similar to those of all other children, so the child will pursue much of the National Curriculum. However, taking a broader view of the child's additional needs might show this to be only partially true.

What is 'integrated' education? The question addressed to ten different individuals is likely to produce as many quite distinct definitions. We are as accustomed to hearing just about every conceivable placement arrangement described by professionals as 'integrated' simply because it is now politically incorrect to admit that as educationalists we knowingly and intentionally segregate. Likewise with 'segregation'; it is no longer possible to use the term to describe any placement arrangement at all, because of the embarrassment surrounding the whole idea that we would ever seriously contemplate such a thing. Hence we have developed a plethora of euphemisms to describe our segregated services.

Failing to notice (Unconsciousness)

That so many special schools are so unlike what we understand a school to be, and that this reality remains invisible to those involved, is not surprising because our assumptions about the needs of the children who attend such schools have become confused.

Within the separate world of 'special' education there is an entirely unconscious conspiracy to view the world as we would wish it to be rather than to accept it for what it is. This phenomenon is not, of course, unique to this field of work but is a feature of the way we function as human beings. It is rooted in our desire to avoid what psychologists call 'cognitive dissonance'. This is a state of mind marked by the holding of values, beliefs and understandings that are inconsistent with one another, and that because of this, lead the individual to become uncomfortable when required to contemplate those discordant ideas in juxtaposition.

Dissonance literally mean chaos, cacophony, disharmony. The dissonance comes about when teachers (psychologists, administrators, etc.) contemplate the mismatch between what they understand (and what conventional ethics requires) to be right for children, alongside what they are required to do for and with those children on a day-to-day basis. What this means for the special school (class or unit) teacher is that children are taught in a (more or less) segregated setting and in usually unpromising class groupings, whilst simultaneously holding the view that such segregation and grouping arrangements are not what those children need. The dissonance this creates in the teacher's mind can only be resolved through a complex process of (entirely unconscious) self-deception.

'Unconsciousness' is an extremely important, though much neglected, aspect of human functioning and without it we would find it impossible to cope with the overwhelming barrage of information we must process during our waking hours. Much of our day-to-day routine functioning occurs on what can best be described as 'automatic pilot', which enables us to do several things at once and hence cope with the often conflicting demands of our daily routine.

Unconscious expectation works through the projection of well-rehearsed prediction upon daily events which generally turn out to be well-founded and which in turn reinforce experience. This means that almost any daily experience may become 'normal' through becoming routine and predictable, and the danger is that the individual will eventually become uncritical of some events which are not desirable.

Psychologists have coined another term to describe this psychological phenomenon – 'habituation' – which means quite simply that any activity or situation which is experienced repetitively and routinely will no longer have the same significance and hence will not evoke the same level of attention or interest. Put differently, our response to such events becomes progressively weaker and eventually marked by complete indifference.

These three universal psychological traits – cognitive dissonance, unconsciousness and habituation – conspire to blunt human perception and responsivity so that what might have initially caused the individual to question and challenge will later evoke no response whatsoever. And yet there may well remain a low-level nagging sense of unease because that which is repressed into the unconscious is not completely eliminated from waking consciousness.

Because such mechanisms are integral to human functioning they operate in all areas of our lives and this, of course, includes our professional lives. That this is so creates difficulties for those who see 'professionalism' as somehow cutting through the chaotic subjectivity of human judgement. The popular idea of the professional is that he or she is 'a specialist with a high degree of intellectual expertise: the ability to apply a special technique or scientific approach to control the physical or social environment' (Miller, 1990). To have to contemplate the reality that the special education professionals are as prone to human error in their work as in their personal lives, should give pause to those who have hitherto placed unquestioning trust in such individuals.

The great debate

The debate over the respective virtues of segregated vs integrated education has gone nowhere during the past 10 to 20 years, mainly because professionals and service planners have opted to try and have their cake and eat it and also because legislation has been just passively enabling rather than actively requiring. In view of the failure of the 1981 Act, the fact that the 1993 Act did not strengthen parental rights to have their child integrated is nothing short of disgraceful.

In May 1992 the British Institute for Learning Disabilities (BILD) sponsored a debate with the motion, 'Special schools should be abolished'. Mary Warnock chaired the event and views were evenly divided. It was disappointing to see so many professionals supporting the line now being taken by Warnock herself that not only should special schools not be abolished but that more children should be in them.

Most professionals have apparently decided that special needs provision is essentially soundly based, needing only minor adjustments at the margins, and that integration for children with significant additional needs is anyway an impossible dream. The upshot of this is that nothing really needs to change except the language we use to describe what we do. Political correctness makes it imperative that we get the language right (especially within earshot of the special needs thought-police) but beyond that nothing really matters very much.

Hence we can place children in segregated schools, special classes and units miles from where they live and claim we are 'integrating' them because there is a programme for visiting mainstream settings for the odd lesson each week. We can also progressively adapt our terminology so as to soften and hopefully obscure any potentially embarrassing lacunae between what we are supposed to think and what we actually think about their potential to fit in and function in a mainstream setting. So the child who is still somewhat furtively referred to as having 'low ability' by the *cognoscenti* in his segregated school, will be characterized for outsiders in reports and conversations as 'developmentally delayed' or 'intellectually challenged'.

For years special schools have engaged in a tokenistic approach to integration merely as a sop to their critics, without the slightest intention that it should develop into any worthwhile curricula or social integration. For instance, one special school employed a full-time teacher to organize its 'taster integration' programme. This involved children visiting a mainstream school once a week for what was presumably viewed as a 'taste' of the real world. The school was rarely, if ever, the child's local school and there was no intention of building towards a fuller participation in the life of the school concerned. This programme would have been more aptly called 'teaser integration'.

The statistics produced periodically by the Centre for Studies of Integration in Education (CSIE) show only a minor shift towards the integration of children from special schools, which might now have been put into reverse following the imposition of the National Curriculum and its related testing programme.

Which model for special needs education?

We each have our own idiosyncratic picture of the world and how it works, which is progressively elaborated as we grow and learn. This overall picture is comprised of a vast array of models, or constructs which are themselves rooted in past and ongoing experience that hopefully enables us to project realistic expectations upon the world of events which are, by and large, confirmed by experience.

So all perception is active in this way and not passive as it is sometimes tempting to believe. In addition to this all human perception is also evaluative and this means that in actively perceiving, the individual is also making judgements about what is experienced along various continua. The implications of this fact of human functioning are profound to say the least. It means that when we become trapped within a very tightly defined construct it is nigh on impossible for us to respond (perceive, apprehend, construe) differently until something quite dramatic occurs.

Paradigms and Paradigm Shifts

Another way of making sense of this pattern of human perception/understanding development is to think of it as Thomas Kuhn has proposed in his book, *The Structure of Scientific Revolutions* (1962). He suggests we look at the way in which scientific understanding evolves, and goes on to makes a distinction between continuous and discontinuous scientific progress in the physical sciences, saying that normal science advances by the gradual accumulation of knowledge that progressively elaborates, extends and articulates a paradigm that already exists. Here a paradigm may be construed as a set of presuppositions or basic beliefs which cohere to explain experienced events.

A topical, although somewhat simplistic example of what is meant here, concerns the French Cartesian view of animals which is that they are mere machines without feelings; mere objects. This national view strongly influences the attitude towards farm animals and the way they are transported for slaughter. Having made the mechanistic assumption, all manner of consequences follow which for the typical Frenchman seem perfectly logical and morally neutral. Had the alternative (typically British) assumption been made, i.e. that animals are sentient creatures and as organisms not entirely unlike human beings, then the French would be saddled with what they see as the hopelessly sentimental British approach and along with it a moral dilemma over the treatment of such creatures. So paradigms are powerful shapers of both belief and expectation and they are also strongly predictive of behaviour.

The point of all this is that in the social as well as the physical sciences people will inevitably operate within a paradigm, the assumptions of which will determine how they make sense of experience. The core ideas, values and beliefs implicit in that paradigm will also determine how they undertake their investigations and hence inevitably circumscribe what might be discovered.

Although it is, perhaps, too simplistic, it might help to see a paradigm as providing the setting conditions for the development of a model for making sense of clients and their needs within a social science context. So a paradigm is a shared perception of the world based on a core set of assumptions and expectations about how the world works. In this sense our paradigm determines and rationalizes our actions. The core set of beliefs implicit in paradigms tell us what is real and what we should expect and this is what makes them truly normative 'because they conceal the very reasons for our actions in the unquestioned assumptions of the paradigm' (Patton, 1975).

That the paradigms we operate within are largely unconscious makes them potentially dangerous, but it is in the nature of paradigms that they are only likely to become available for conscious reflection when they are in the process of changing. A further feature of paradigms is that they exist at varying levels of abstraction and Skrtic (1991) describes this in the following way:

> Thus, a scientific community engaged in normal science can be understood as operating on the basis of a hierarchy of implicit presuppositions, which from most to least abstract, include metatheories, theories, assumptions, models, practices, and tools, each of which are defined and subsumed by the higher levels in the hierarchy of abstraction, and all of which, ultimately, are defined and subsumed by the metaphysical paradigm.

Models within paradigms

Although the work of Kuhn in 1962 (from which the notions of paradigm and paradigm shift are drawn) was concerned with the physical sciences, the concepts are equally applicable to the social sciences. The application of this way of thinking (about our deeply ingrained beliefs and understandings) to particular areas of professional practice is far from unproblematic, but it is possible to discern certain significant core assumptions through the imposition of certain (albeit stereotypical) theoretical models on working practice to see whether their predictions are reflected in day-to-day practice.

The medical model

It is increasingly argued that the special education paradigm is still largely rooted in the medical model of disability which views the child or young person as sick or broken and hence in need of being made well or whole once more. Furthermore from within the medical model the disabled or learning impaired child is seen as the problem who must adapt or be adapted to suit the requirements of the world as it is for non-disabled children. Linked to this is an approach to service development which sees the child as 'special' or 'different', since he or she requires additional or different resources which are to be largely provided by specialist professionals in separate settings. It is this medical model view which created the large institutions and which still permeates much of the thinking and day-to-day practice of special needs professionals.

The test of whether a particular professional or service is operating within a paradigm (of what it is to be human) which embodies the medical model is at root quite a simple one which concerns the perceived focus of the need to change. If it is being constantly suggested that the impaired individual must change, then there is clear evidence of a medical model assumption.

The social model

The social model of disability takes as its starting point that serious illness and physical or intellectual impairment exist, but only become disabling because of the rejecting and oppressive response to such impairments by the non-disabled world. Advocates of the social model (largely physically disabled persons and their allies) argue that the answer to the problem of disability lies in the restructuring of social attitudes and the physical environment. The core assumptions of the social model are best expressed by the statement that 'people with disabilities are limited more by the attitudes of others than by their physical or intellectual impairments'.

The argument then, is that special education is stuck within a completely inappropriate and highly damaging paradigm (or model) because it is one which has lead to a highly negative perception of the children to be served; also that this has resulted in a variety of unhelpful, if not damaging, practices. It is, therefore, time for a complete rethink of the role of special education and a major paradigm shift. Such a major rethink should, of course, equally be applied to services for adults with impairments which result in their being socially devalued.

Normalization/social role valorization

The term 'normalization' is not a part of the lexicon of most educationalists, although it has become a byword for the development of community-based services for adults with learning difficulties. The most influential formulation of the theory has been developed by Wolf Wolfensberger (1972) who has also devised two instruments for assessing the effectiveness of services in meeting normalization related criteria (PASS and PASSING).

The starting point for normalization is an understanding of the historical position of people who have a learning difficulty or physical disability, or who for some other reason have suffered social rejection and isolation. Within the theory, such individuals or groups have been seen as having low social status through having had a low value placed upon them because of their possession of characteristics which are themselves devalued within their society.

Human characteristics likely to be only mildly societally devalued are many and varied, and may also differ between societies or cultures. Likewise, a particular characteristic might be valued at one time and devalued at another. Here we might be referring to such relatively trivial characteristics such as the size of a person's nose or feet, or their general bodily shape or even the colour of their hair or its absence. The possession of such characteristics, whilst not being socially valued, will not lead to a significant social devaluation of the individual as would the case were they to possess a significant visible impairment. Individuals with a major physical or sensory impairment or a severe learning difficulty are at major risk of being devalued irrespective of the society they live in.

Severe physical disabilities and significant learning difficulties tend to be fairly universally devalued, although even here there are differential tolerance levels across cultures. The elderly are also at increasing risk of social rejection especially if they become disabled or disordered in their thinking.

Following a period during which a number of misunderstandings became attached to the term normalization, Wolfensberger was also developing his understanding of the key elements of social devaluation. He came to see that the essential defining characteristics of social acceptance and high social status were concerned with the individual's ability to fulfil a variety of valued social roles. The obverse of this was of course that those individuals who had few or only lowly valued social roles were placed at far greater risk of societal rejection, isolation, exploitation and possibly even physical harm.

The paradigm (of what it is to be human) implicit within normalization theory is more ambiguous than that for the medical or social models. There is a conservatism in its analysis that strenuous efforts should be made to support the devalued individual's social acceptance which is sometimes seen as a pandering to the norms of a rejecting society rather than challenging its insularity.

In truth, normalization (or social role valorization) is a body of research which has done a great deal to highlight the underlying social dynamic of social devaluation and rejection but which needs to be treated with caution in respect of its recommendations for reversing this process.

So what does all this depressing stuff have to do with the elaboration of a paradigm for special education? Well, just about everything – let me explain.

Deviancy-making in Special Education

If a valued individual spends time alongside other valued people doing socially valued things in valued social settings, then the exact reverse is the case for those upon whom a low social value has been placed.

To be systematically excluded from the company of socially valued others and the places they inhabit poses a very real danger for a person who possesses observable characteristics which are known to be socially devalued. This exclusion implies also that the individual is relegated to a social milieu which can only serve to compound the disadvantages the individual already has. To be removed from the mainstream of community life represents the most damning judgement of one's peers on one's human worth in that at root it represents a questioning of that individual's human status.

In most modern states, an individual is only involuntarily separated from society if he or she is judged to be a danger to themself or to others. There are all manner of legal safeguards in place to protect the right of the individual not to be segregated. No such rights exist for approximately 3 per cent of children who experience enforced educational segregation. This is not to say that all of the parents of these children would choose a mainstream place if they were given a genuine choice, but rather that current legislation does not allow them such a choice.

As far as schooling is concerned, most parents choose to send their children to the local school to follow the curriculum alongside other children who share their local community. It would be fair to say that this is what we mean by a socially valued educational experience. The reason we say this is socially valued is simply because most people choose it for their children and, because they choose it, they presumably value it.

This model for schooling is very different to what the special school has to offer. The question we then need to ask of the special school, special class or unit is – does it provide a socially valued education for the children it serves? The answer is, of course, no! The reason for this is first and foremost that it is not something which most parents would choose for their child were they to be offered a genuine choice. It is more likely to be accepted as the least-worst option.

If judged by these criteria, does the school provide an opportunity to be with valued others, doing valued things? In the course of developing a valued role, the segregated school or class fails the test. Again it is important to stress that the model being used here is that for a child with a severe disability and complex needs such that at present he or she would probably be placed in a segregated setting.

Special school practice

Because special schools have historically developed their curricula within the medical model paradigm, they have tended to pursue what might be called a 'therapeutic' rather than an 'educational' curriculum. This therapy orientation is marked by an obsessive attention to functional deficits in learners linked to a 'treatment' approach which results in largely futile attempts to 'fix' that which is essentially non-fixable. In schools for children with severe and complex disabilities, this has involved such speculative endeavours as aromatherapy, snoezelen (multi-sensory stimulation) therapy, rebound therapy (trampolining) and horse-riding (hippo therapy) etc. which, because they are conceived as therapeutic interventions, focus attention upon the perceived need to 'cure' rather than to educate. It is not surprising that within such a medically-oriented paradigm the social aspects of education are relegated to a minor role.

Research on the work of segregated schools might reveal a positive correlation between a therapeutic curriculum and a lack of concern for social integration. Segregation brings with it a plethora of additional disadvantages for pupils, including poor role models, negative labelling, age- and need-inappropriate grouping, unnecessary travelling and social isolation. The most frequently cited justification for all of this is that separation is necessary if the pupil is to have his or her most pressing needs met. Here the reference is to the teaching expertise and the availability of paramedical staff offering speech, physio and occupational therapy, etc. and the greater likelihood of there being a nurse on the staff who can act on medical needs.

That such support could and should be made available in mainstream settings does not wash with those who see the virtues of the segregated setting. This uncritical acceptance of a medical model solution to educating large numbers of vulnerable children is based upon a major misunderstanding of the needs of children.

Fundamental vs Additional needs

It is important for SEN professionals to distinguish between a child's fundamental developmental needs and any additional needs he or she may have as a consequence of a particular impairment or difficulty. Much is said and written about the needs of children, and during recent years there has been a significant increase in the pace and weight of legislation aimed at securing the rights of different groups of children and to more effectively meeting their needs. We have seen the Children Act (1989) and the 1993

Education Act introduce what are intended to be major safeguards for vulnerable children in a social climate in which children appear to be increasingly at risk. Yet when it comes to organizing professional services to put in place such safeguards serious misunderstandings get in the way. That all children have a shared set of fundamental needs tends to be overlooked when it comes to organizing an education service for that minority who have some important additional needs.

It is readily acknowledged and goes without saying that our education service must operate on the basis of positive discrimination towards children with significant additional needs. However, in spite of our universal acceptance of this principle we continue, unnecessarily, to disadvantage a significant minority of pupils by our failure to distinguish between that which is fundamental and that which, in spite of being very important, is merely additional, and this is because we become perceptually dominated by the difference.

A practical example of this key distinction is available if we look at a child's home-to-school transport needs. Any child will need a comfortable form of seating and a bodily restraint system within a safe vehicle. A disabled child will need just this but the exact form in which the provision is made may require an adapted seat and harness and perhaps a vehicle which has itself undergone extensive adaptations to provide a lift and floor tracking for wheelchairs, etc. The fundamental needs of each child for secure and comfortable home-to-school transport are identical but the way in which those needs must be provided for are very different.

This same principle is, of course, applicable to the curriculum but teachers have a mental block about this because they have little experience of children who are atypical.

Why specialists keep getting it wrong

Special needs professionals must discipline themselves to be less precious about their skills and get back to some simple child development fundamentals. One useful starting point is a little book written 20 years ago by Mia Kellmer Pringle (*The Needs of Children*, 1975) the then Director of the National Children's Bureau. In this book she said that all children share some very basic needs which are for love and security, new experiences, recognition and achievement, and the taking of responsibility. She went on to say that:

> How well a handicapped child makes out in the long run depends far less on the nature, severity or onset of his condition than on the attitudes of his

parents first and foremost, then on those of his peers and teachers, and eventually on society's. These determine how he feels about his handicap.

If we can assume that the family provides the love and security then it is not unreasonable to expect that the school should provide a model of good educational practice in developing the other key needs through its curriculum, whilst providing the family with an appropriate model for how this should be tackled. The segregated class or special school does not offer such a model.

It may seem hard on that diverse group of individuals – the special needs professionals – to keep banging on about how badly they have got it wrong, but they really have and this fact is not without consequence for many children and their families. For them now to be able to start getting it right requires a major perceptual shift of the kind I have described, which in turn implies extensive retraining.

'Special' education – A label without a rationale

We have seen that the failure to distinguish between fundamental and additional needs is in large part due to a failure to understand what the real needs of disabled children are. We have also seen that this failure is itself caused by an adoption of the wrong paradigm. One consequence of working within the wrong paradigm has been that the practice of 'special' education has developed out of a professional desire to find out more and more about less and less of the child's dysfunctionality and, as we have seen, an unfortunate corollary of this has been that children have been subjected to practices more likely to retard than promote their development.

The willingness of the special needs professional to adopt the role of 'deviancy manager' rather than educationalist *per se*, says more about the extent to which they have internalized the medical model paradigm than about the real needs of children and young people they are paid to serve.

That there is not an identifiably separate discipline of 'special' education testifies to the fact that we have not yet developed a credible set of techniques, strategies, interventions or whatever, which could be seen to represent a coherent body of professional knowledge. The (usually implicit) assumption that this is what is indeed happening can only work to the disadvantage of children with SEN, because the existence of a separate educational discipline specifically to meet their needs would need to show that the way they learn is essentially different from the way most other children learn, and this in turn would be used to support the case for separate places.

The professionalization of special needs education has, for good or ill, filled the lives of children with specialists, and to the extent that they are involved in meeting genuine needs this is to be welcomed. A danger though, is that the presence of these people will serve to drive out ordinary people who may come to believe that you need to be an 'expert' to spend time usefully with a child who has such extensive additional needs.

Fundamental needs: reviewing for relevance

Since it is a central point of this chapter that the honest endeavour to meet 'special' (additional) needs has got in the way of our being able to meet fundamental needs, it is important to offer evidence from the segregated setting itself.

One simple technique which more than any other serves to highlight the dangers inherent in segregation (and the medicalization of impairment) is known as the Circle of Relationships. The author has used this technique as part of a broader review strategy for identifying the needs of children who attend segregated schools.

With a small group of family connections and key professionals, a facilitator draws four concentric circles on the board as shown in Figure 9.1. The name of the child concerned is placed in the middle of the central circle, and those present are asked to identify those people who are involved in an intimate, mutually loving relationship with the child; this is usually though not exclusively the immediate family. This process is then repeated for the remaining circles 2–4 where the aim is to identify: friends, acquaintances and professionals. For children with a severe disability this usually produces a picture somewhat like that in Figure 9.2. The next step is to relate this information to the picture achieved by asking the group to address the following questions about the child concerned:

Who is X?
What are his main needs?
Where can those needs best be met?
What means should be employed to meet his needs?
Who should be involved in meeting those needs?
With whom should X be grouped to have his needs met?

Asking who the child is is not as redundant as it might at first appear, since children with severe disabilities have attracted all manner of professional labels which may serve to distort the way they are perceived

96

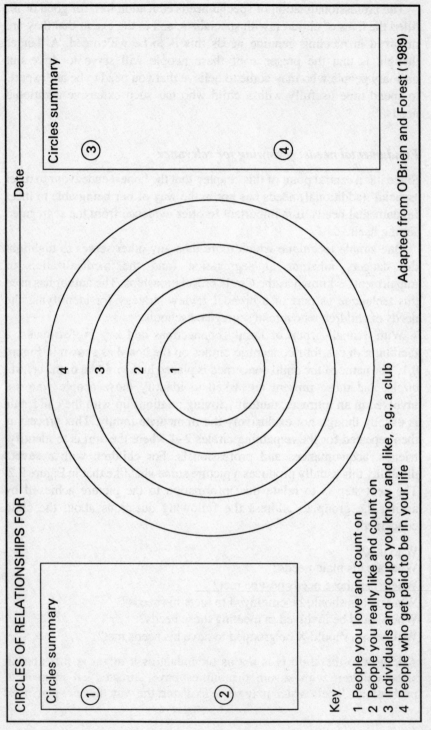

Figure 9.1 The circles of relationships

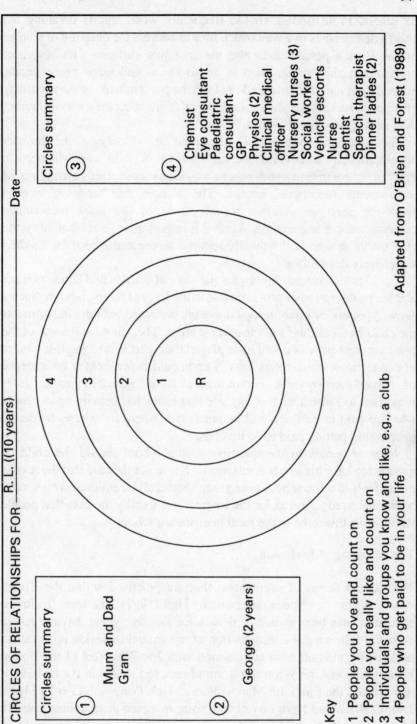

CIRCLES OF RELATIONSHIPS FOR ___ R.L. ((10 years) _____ Date _____

Circles summary

① Mum and Dad
   Gran

② George (2 years)

③

④ Chemist
   Eye consultant
   Paediatric
   consultant
   GP
   Physios (2)
   Clinical medical
   officer
   Nursery nurses (3)
   Social worker
   Vehicle escorts
   Nurse
   Dentist
   Speech therapist
   Dinner ladies (2)

Key

1 People you love and count on
2 People you really like and count on
3 Individuals and groups you know and like, e.g., a club
4 People who get paid to be in your life

Adapted from O'Brien and Forest (1989)

Figure 9.2 Completed circles of relationships

by others. Professionals all too frequently write reports detailing the child's deficiencies in a way which fails to address the question of who he or she is as a person. It is also the case that children with severe or profound disabilities are hard to get to know, and many professionals either do not have the time or do not see the point in making the necessary effort because they see their role as one of 'delivering their service' rather than getting to know the child.

The question about needs is aimed at identifying the broader developmental needs (fundamental needs) of a child who will need to grow up in community with others, as well as those needs arising out of impairments (additional needs). The picture that tends to emerge following such an analysis reveals some of the most problematic consequences of segregation. Again it is important to stress that this is the case for those who will typically attend a segregated school for children with severe disabilities.

The Circles exercise highlights the lack of friends and acquaintances and the proliferation of professionals in the lives of these children. Such a skewed pattern of relationships is not unconnected with the impairments the child has, but this is not the whole story. The school and some of the other services provided will have played their part in creating this pattern of connections which relies heavily upon paid expert help at the expense of natural freely-given commitments from ordinary people. It is important to remember that any life that relies too heavily upon people who are paid to be there will be put at risk when, for whatever reason, people stop getting paid to be involved.

When it comes to the question – with whom should the child be grouped to have his or her needs met? – it is never the case that the review group feels that the school peer group should all be children with similar additional needs. And as for the where?, it is usually the case that people would wish this to be in the local mainstream school.

The Meaning of Inclusion

The various forms of segregation that are practised within the British school system have been described by Hall (1992). The term 'inclusive education' has been in use in Britain for just five years, having gained currency following the introduction of the annual inclusion conferences initiated by the author in conjunction with Joe Whittaker of the Bolton Institute. It was Joe Whittaker's initial visit to Canada in the late 1980s that created the link with Marsha Forest, Jack Pearpoint, George Flynn, John O'Brien and Herb Lovett who were involved in an annual event at McGill University in Montreal.

The term 'inclusion' began to be used as a more precise way of describing what British educationalists had called 'functional integration' i.e. integration which involved the child with special needs having a curricular, rather than merely a social, involvement with his mainstream peers. But the term inclusion embraced a much deeper philosophical notion of what integration should mean and in this sense was truly prescriptive.

The best way to characterize this difference is by noting that in Britain commentators merely observed the various kinds of integration they saw about them and coined terms which served to describe what was happening, hence:

Social integration meant children with SEN mixing at break times.

Locational integration meant they were on the same school campus but pursuing a separate curriculum in a separate classroom.

Functional integration meant full participation (or at least as much as was deemed possible) in the ordinary classroom.

It was very different with the introduction of the term 'inclusive education', which was rooted in prescription rather than description. The North American proponents of full inclusion for all children took as their starting point that it is a matter of basic human rights that children should not be excluded from the educational mainstream. So, from the outset, the meaning of inclusion is linked to notions of social justice and community presence and participation.

There is no firm agreement on definitions, but taking account of the key elements of the social justice argument and linking this to the best practice that has emerged in North America, the author would offer the following as the basis of a working definition. To be fully included in the educational mainstream means:

> *Being a full member of an age-appropriate class in your local school doing the same lessons as the other pupils and it mattering if you are not there. Plus you have friends who spend time with you outside school.*

Such definitions are inevitably arbitrary, although the key elements are not negotiable. This definition makes it clear to the school that their role is much broader than merely ensuring that the child has a programme of work in an ordinary classroom. It does this by highlighting the following key issues.

Age-appropriateness

This is indeed a key issue for people with learning difficulties who tend to be treated age-inappropriately because it is believed that an individual's mental age is measurable and furthermore that it provides a guide as to how they should be approached.

It is important to relate to all children, and most especially to those with learning difficulties, in an age-appropriate manner otherwise they may well fulfil the lower expectation you place upon them. In the case of an expectation that would be appropriate for a much younger child, this would lead not only to age-inappropriate behaviour on the occasion in question but to the internalization of the idea that 'other people want me to behave like a younger child'. It is easier for all children to engage in age-inappropriate behaviour which reflects a lower than a higher chronological age.

Local school presence

Attending the school which serves the local community is, as we have seen, a socially valued thing to do. The value most people would identify is that it enables children to get to know each other and carry over those friendships into their lives outside school. Being included in school makes it less likely that a child will be excluded outside of school, and vice versa.

Sharing lessons

Being accepted and included requires both physical presence and participation. Any lesson can be interpreted for any child so as to make such participation meaningful. Being physically present in the classroom creates the opportunity for interactions which would never occur if the child attended another school (perhaps a special school) in another part of town.

Making friendships and developing understanding

Getting to know others is not something thought worthy of planning for or measuring in our schools. This is what we have tended to call 'the hidden curriculum', which embraces those thousand and one interpersonal encounters, observations and other informal experiences that make up the typical school day.

Learning what your peers wear, how they behave, what they like, what they aspire to; learning how adults other than your own parents relate to children; learning how to make and break friendships and what the power structure is within the school – these and many other learning opportunities are presented to children in school but most are not on offer in a segregated special school.

Community competence

As well as denying opportunities to their own pupils, special schools serve also to undermine a key learning opportunity for all other children. They do this by ensuring that a minority of children spend their school years out of contact with their typical peers who then cannot get to know them. That severely disabled children remain forever mysterious to most others in society is due in large part to the fact that are absent from the places where most people spend their time.

Getting to know how another human being without speech is able to communicate; learning how a child with little or no use of his limbs needs to be cared for and supported to learn; discovering how a person with a learning difficulty can begin to understand if taught differently – all of these opportunities are denied to children in mainstream schools. These lost opportunities to learn undermine the competence of whole communities to help vulnerable people. Perhaps most damaging of all is the lost opportunity for friendships to develop. If schools and colleges were to become inclusive, they would set a better example to society of the way it should order itself.

Finally, it is probably important to offer a health warning to anyone who might be tempted to splash out their hard-earned money on a workshop or conference on inclusive education. Do by all means go along and listen to what the speakers have to say, but be just a little wary if someone tells you that it is easy to get a child included. There remain powerful societal forces resisting the inclusion of many children in the educational mainstream, not the least important of which is the attitudes of professionals who have a powerful vested interest in the status quo. It is important to remember, though, that professionals work to a mandate defined by the larger society, and it is here that a major shift in understanding is now required.

References

Hall, J.T. (1992) 'Token integration: how can we explain such odd practices', *Learning Together Magazine*, No. 3.
Kellmer-Pringle, M.(1975) *The Needs of Children*, London: Hutchingson.
Kuhn, T.S. (1962) *The Structure of Scientific Revolutions*, Chicago, IL: University of Chicago Press.

102

Miller, R. (1990) *What are Schools for? Holistic education in American culture*, Brandon, VT: Holistic Education Press.

O'Brien, J. and Forest, M. (1989) *Action for Inclusion: How to improve schools by welcoming children with special needs into regular classrooms*, Toronto: Inclusion Press.

Patton, M.Q. (1975) *Alternative Evaluation Research Paradigm*, Grand Forks, ND: University of North Dakota Press.

Skrtic, T.M. (1991) *Behind Special Education*, Denver, CO: Love Publishing Company.

Wolfensberger, W. (1972) *The Principle of Normalisation in Human Services*, Toronto: National Institute on Mental Retardation.

Wolfensberger, W. and Glenn, L. (1975) *Programme Analysis of Service Systems, A method for the quantitative analysis of human services.(PASS) Vol I Handbook, Vol II Field Manual*, (2nd edn) Toronto: National Institute on Mental Retardation, 1975, reprinted 1978.

Wolfensberger, W. and Thomas, S. (1983) *PASSING (Programme Analysis of Service Systems Implementation of Normalisation Goals), Normalisation criteria and ratings manual*, (2nd edn) Toronto: National Institute on Mental Retardation.

CHAPTER 8

Integration and Education: Theory and Practice

Pat Conway and Paul Baker

Introduction

We are currently witnessing a move in educational policy and practice in England and Wales towards integrating pupils with severe learning difficulties into mainstream schools (a similar move is happening in Scotland too, though under different legislation). The momentum can be seen as being inspired by the 1981 Education Act, based mainly on the Warnock Report (DES, 1978). The 1993 Education Act (Code of Practice) recognizes, as a principle, that there needs to be a consortium of provision to meet special educational needs (SEN) and, whenever possible, pupils should be educated in mainstream schools.

This chapter sets out to explore current issues in the debate on integration in England and Wales and to use this exploration as a stimulus for discussion. This educationally-based discussion will be placed in the context of an overall philosophical view of integration encompassing social justice, civil rights and equality. Indeed, *equality* in terms of human rights has been the driving force behind many integration initiatives. However, integration also encompasses the concept of *educational equality* and, as such, requires a fundamental set of principles which, if based on educational and related theories, would ensure that practices in integration are educationally sound. Here in the UK there appears to be a lack of theoretical evidence to support integration as educationally and psychologically sound. Instead there seem to be many *laissez-faire* policies couched in psychological jargon and misleading assumptions, all aiming for 'full' integration.

The evidence provided by theory and research in the UK and USA (where there is a longer history of integration) will play a central part in the discussion in this chapter, alongside descriptions of types of integration currently experienced by pupils with differing educational needs.

The Practice of Integration

Many pupils with SEN are currently on the roll of mainstream schools. Because of their placement, it may be assumed that they are 'integrated'. However, as we shall go on to discuss later, this is not necessarily the case. Are mainstream schools adequately prepared and resourced to educate pupils with varying types of learning difficulties? Alternatively, are they recreating microcosms of a segregated system 'hidden' behind a wall of assumptions which is already toppling over and burying the educational and social needs of the very pupils we aim to integrate?

There is, of course, a great diversity of need amongst pupils with profound and multiple (PMLD) and severe (SLD) learning difficulties. Furthermore, in many respects, distinctions between these groups and between them and pupils with moderate learning difficulties (MLD) and physical disabilities (PD) may be more bureaucratic than real. However, for the purposes of this chapter, current practice for each of these groups of pupils will be considered separately.

Pupils with Profound and Multiple Learning Difficulties

Whilst pupils who present with PMLD are usually educated in SLD schools, they have traditionally been educated in separate groups. Ouvry (1986) referred to this group as suffering a 'double segregation': segregated within a special school, and then further segregated in a special class or unit. Increasingly, though, since the mid-1980, pupils with PMLD have been integrated into classes within the SLD school with their peers, so that now it is thought that about 50 per cent of pupils with PMLD are integrated into SLD classes. There are a small number of examples of students with PMLD being integrated into mainstream classrooms (e.g. Austin and Gathercole, 1989; Toon, 1988), although little research has been carried out in this area. One final type of integration which will affect an increasing number of pupils with PMLD is often called 'link integration'. This is where a class or group from an SLD class spends time as a group in a mainstream school. (This is described further in the following section on pupils with SLD.)

Pupils with PMLD require therapeutic input from a range of professionals such as speech and language therapists, physiotherapists and occupational therapists, as well as the extension and continuation of this therapy by teachers. They have traditionally had greater access to educational professionals, with an emphasis on individual learning programmes through individual teaching and the development of highly individualized learning goals. There have been few attempts to develop a qualification for teachers of pupils with PMLD, since they represent a small minority of SLD teachers, thus making course development uncommercial. However, there has been a growing trend to develop curriculum material and short courses for teachers, particularly in the development of multi-sensory work and the development of cognition and communication. It must also be said that these pupils frequently do not receive the level of therapeutic support they need, since scarcity of resources often affects them disproportionately.

The curriculum for pupils with PMLD, whilst incorporating the National Curriculum, has placed great emphasis on cognition, communication, perceptual and sensory development, and on developing physical and self-help skills. This is motivated by the nature and complexity of their disabilities, which combine profound learning difficulties with a range of physical, sensory and perceptual impairments that often results in a disability that challenges even the most skilful teacher. This has led to the evolution of a multidisciplinary approach being used to both develop and deliver the curriculum and therapy. Since these pupils learn at a very slow rate, their achievements can appear very limited.

The main objective given in the literature for integrating these pupils is social (Ouvry, 1986); this seems to be reasonable but is not an easy area to evaluate. The National Curriculum is rarely seen as wholly appropriate for these pupils, with many SLD teachers expressing feelings of inadequacy when devising or implementing curricula programmes of study and schemes of work (Humphreys, 1994). It is not unusual for many pupils with PMLD to appear 'curricularly isolated' when integrated into an SLD classroom full time. Their needs tend to be met apart from their peers, both because of the difference in their needs, and also the demands of their more vocal and able classmates. This situation was noted by Evans and Ware (1987), who saw the integration of pupils with PMLD into SLD classrooms as probably making the situation worse for these pupils in terms of the curriculum meeting their individual needs.

From the limited evidence available, it would appear that the integration of pupils with PMLD needs to be evaluated far more rigorously than at present. The commitment to provide for their curricular needs has implications for the training and professional development of all members of staff in SLD schools. The specific educational goals of each pupil need to be defined, so that the notion of a social objective for integration within an SLD classroom is not made either the most important or only objective, as appears to be the case at present. Finally, there has to be a rigorous evaluation based on how effectively the pupil is learning and whether they are receiving adequate therapeutic input.

Pupils with Severe Learning Difficulties

Pupils with SLD, because of the nature of their learning difficulties, need a curriculum that is presented in small steps and which addresses a wider range of areas than the usual academic curriculum. The development of communication and problem-solving take a priority place, along with the development of a range of social and independent learning skills which assists in making the National Curriculum accessible.

The SLD school has available the experience of teachers, some of whom will have an additional qualification in the education of pupils with SLD, along with classroom assistants and therapists who will have developed expertise in this area. One worrying trend for pupils fully integrated into mainstream schools is the provision of support by untrained and usually unqualified classroom assistants. This pattern of provision may be supplemented by advice and support from a teacher qualified in the education of pupils with SLD. Nevertheless, it seems to place a considerable burden on the mainstream class teacher and special needs coordinator.

Integration for pupils with SLD is experienced in a great diversity of ways, with virtually all pupils involved in some form of integration. The three objectives described in much of the literature (e.g., Carpenter *et al.*, 1991) are social integration, experiential integration and curricular integration. It is possible to identify programmes which offer each of these to pupils with SLD. Link schemes, for instance, allow whole classes or groups to link with classes in neighbouring mainstream schools, usually to participate in lessons such as music, PE or art. Alternatively, a growing number of individual programmes place pupils on the full-time roll of mainstream schools. Further aspects of integration are work experience and links with appropriate courses at colleges of further education.

Research suggests that most pupils with SLD have some contact with their mainstream peers (Toon, 1988). The most able are generally given a programme which allows them to study full-time with their peers at primary level; yet as they get older, and the gap between their achievements and those of their classmates widens, there is a greater probability of their returning to a special school (Austin and Gathercole, 1989). Few pupils are integrated full-time into high schools. Indeed, there is increasing evidence (Tilstone, 1991) that many pupils with SLD, after experiencing a high degree of integration at primary schools, will return to segregated special schools when they reach secondary school age (11 years). This raises obvious questions about the effect such a transition has on the pupil, as well as the effects on both parents and teachers.

Pupils with Moderate Learning Difficulties

As Samson and Reason (1988) note, the term 'moderate learning difficulties' as used in England and Wales is a relative term, and is used to describe pupils whose learning difficulties do not usually become apparent until they have been at school for a few years and have failed to learn effectively in the mainstream system. There are no reliable statistics to indicate how many children are considered to have MLD, although Williams (1993) suggests that it is '… roughly two percent of the school population…'; and since there are no reliable statistics or numbers, we have little understanding of how many pupils with MLD have been reintegrated. It is important to make the distinction noted by Samson and Reason (op. cit.) that, since these are essentially pupils whom the mainstream system has decided it can not educate, any movement back to mainstream schools is reintegration and not integration. Williams (op. cit.) makes two further points which we need to take note of when defining the group. First, pupils with MLD show a high incidence of associated difficulties, particularly speech and language difficulties and behavioural and emotional difficulties. Second, there is an over-representation of children from low income groups and ethnic minorities. Perhaps the integration of pupils with MLD is the acid test of integration policies, since they constitute the largest group of pupils in segregated education and receive less sympathy than pupils with physical or sensory disabilities.

The majority of pupils with MLD seem to be educated in separate special schools, but a number of mainstream schools have units for such pupils attached to them – a concept many seem to be unhappy with. However, far from being seen as a mid-point towards full integration, Martlew and Hodson (1991) suggest that pupils in units tend to be more socially isolated and are teased and bullied more frequently by their peers. The present pattern of integration lays emphasis on returning pupils to full-time mainstream education, although Sheldon (1991), amongst others, notes the increasing difficulty of integrating pupils as they get older. Williams (1993) cites a number of examples of different patterns of integration, but in general they may all be seen to lead towards full-time reintegration into mainstream schools.

In common with our earlier comments, integration for pupils with MLD is often justified in terms of social needs, in particular the repairing of self-esteem associated with rejection by school. Yet there is some research data which looks closely at academic performance as well as other areas, such as behaviour. Samson and Reason (1988) note that since pupils were transferred from mainstream schools because they were not learning effectively, on reintegrating, even if they receive a lot of support from the mainstream schools special needs departments, they can still be seen to be achieving academically if they are able to cope. This echoes a point made by Smith and Goldthorpe (1988) that the pupils' achievements must be seen within the context of their coping with the school and recognizing their own achievement. Interestingly, many professionals see the role of the MLD school as Sheldon (1991) does: mainly as one of repairing the pupils' self-esteem, helping them to learn basic skills (particularly reading and writing) and then giving them a range of social coping skills to help them survive in mainstream school. It may, therefore, be realistic to say that academic survival rather than academic success would be a realistic criteria for judging the effectiveness of MLD integration programmes.

The need for expertise within the mainstream school is noted in much of the research, and both Smith and Goldthorpe (1988) and Samson and Reason (1988) emphasize that this means access to a differentiated curriculum which allows the pupil with MLD to experience success in learning. The recent development of the National Curriculum in England and Wales makes it possible to develop curriculum links between the special school and the mainstream school. This will serve to enhance the possibility of successful reintegration. Equally important has been the development in mainstream schools of a variety of support strategies for pupils experiencing learning difficulties. In particular, the development of support teaching and 'in-class' support means that mainstream class teachers are given the opportunity to develop their own skills without being concerned that other pupils are becoming pedagogically neglected.

In concluding this section, we must emphasize some problems. The first is the lack of a clear and accepted definition of 'moderate learning difficulties' which results in confusion as to who, exactly, is qualified to fit into this category. The second problem is the tendency, by local education authorities, to place pupils with 'emotional and behavioural difficulties' in MLD schools. Thus, the basic aim of enhancing social and coping skills becomes harder to achieve.

Pupils with Physical Disabilities

Children with PD have been placed on the roll of mainstream schools in increasing numbers over the past ten years. There has been a corresponding decrease in the number of special schools catering for this group of pupils. Initially, as Jacklin and Lacey (1991) note, the pupils transferred were those with minimal disabilities and also those who were most capable both intellectually, emotionally and physically. But as the provision of technical support has improved, and mainstream schools have been able to overcome problems of physical accessibility, pupils with more severe disabilities have been integrated. This has led to special schools which are educating a smaller number of pupils with more severe and, in many cases, more complex impairments (Lonton and Farooqui, 1991).

In considering expertise for this group of pupils, provision of medical and therapeutic skills must be addressed. The process is not simply one of integration, but also one of 'desegregation' for the special school. This means structuring support into outreach networks, and meeting the many concerns and training needs of the school the pupil is being integrated into. These concerns range from the need for clear factual information on the care and needs of these pupils, through to fears about bullying; overall the literature makes it clear that these fears are largely unfounded (Bailey, 1988). There also needs to be a careful evaluation of the types of support that the school, family and pupil require to enable them to move away from the over-protective structures which have been characteristic of special schools in the past.

The research indicates that a high percentage of pupils with PD are experiencing some form of integration, ranging from the complete integration outlined by Jacklin and Lacey (1991) to the part-time and social integration noted by Howarth (1987). A major concern of Gibb and Donkersloot (1991) is the need to see the integration of pupils with PD as a highly individual enterprise, which takes into account their emotional needs, their academic and social development, and the type of support they will need in their mainstream school. Lalkhen and Norwich (1990) suggest that the pupil should be prepared for the integration process through the use of carefully structured integration experiences within which the views of the pupil are sought, considered important and have influence.

Stukat (1993) notes that much of the research has centred on the success of the social process of integration, whilst ignoring academic outcomes. It would seem that for any integration process to be evaluated accurately, academic needs and outcomes must be evaluated as critically as emotional and physical needs. More than any other group of pupils with special educational needs, the process of integrating pupils with PD has been characterized by positive attitudes and experiences. For this to continue, Stukat points out that we need to address our research efforts to the educational feasibility of integration, to ensure that social and emotional successes are not gained at the expense of the pupils' education.

The Theory of Integration

Two theories which might help to dispel commonly held assumptions about integration are social learning theory (Bandura, 1977) and the contact hypothesis (Allport, 1954). Integration from an educational perspective is often based on certain assumptions, for example that placing pupils with SEN into mainstream schools automatically means that they are integrated. The available evidence does not support this assumption. It is also assumed that pupils with SEN automatically imitate models of good behaviour from mainstream peers. This assumption, too, lacks support. Is it good behaviour that integrationists are after, or more sophisticated behaviour, e.g. better communicative skills or social interaction skills? General educational jargon has been emptied into the melting pot of integration, losing any credibility, being totally misconstrued. For example, we hear a great number of references to modelling from pro-integrationists at all levels, and from all corners. These imply that pupils with SLD automatically imitate 'good behaviour' both socially and in learning from their mainstream peers. This is not necessarily so and is quite a dangerous assumption, as it implies that pupils with SLD do not exhibit good behaviour models themselves and do not have access to such models in special schools. Modelling, a concept derived from social learning theory does not happen spontaneously but only under certain conditions. As Stobart (1986) explains, integration is more than just placing pupils with SEN and their mainstream peers together, and that contact, delabelling and modelling are not simple and magical formulae which operate under *laissez faire* conditions. If integration is to be educationally justifiable, it must operate within structures, settings and conditions which have been empirically proven, within a wider context which promotes and reflects true equality of social justice, civil and human rights. The first step of the integration process is placement. How often do we think that we have 'achieved' integration just by placing pupils with SLD alongside their mainstream peers, within mainstream schools?

The contact hypothesis (Allport, 1954) states that, of itself, physical placement of people in close proximity without regard for differences such as race, colour or national origin is not sufficient to destroy negative stereotypes and develop positive attitudes. If this is the case, what are the implications for integration which has been preceded by 100 years of segregation encased with negative attitudes and negative stereotypes of people with learning difficulties? Placement alone does not complete the integration process. The contact hypothesis states that when groups of human beings meet they normally pass through four stages of relationship, these stages appear to relate closely to the integration process:

The contact hypothesis: stages of relationships		Integration
1. Sheer contact	– not integration	Placement
2. Competition	– not integration	Some social activities Competitive games
3. Accommodation	– not integration	Special classes,units, links
4. Assimilation	– integration achieved	Full integration (educational and social)

These stages are also reversible. Settings can be created which encourage pupils to reach the assimilation stage, without 'sticking' at the previous stages, or allowing retrogression to occur, which would fall short of integration. As contact between pupils with SLD and their mainstream peers occurs in social and academic settings, it is important that such contact is reached and maintained at the assimilation level in both areas.

Social integration (e.g., playground, dinner, youth clubs) is the setting which puts pupils with SLD at risk in terms of not developing beyond the sheer contact stage. There is a large body of research which suggests that interactions between pupils with SLD and their mainstream peers are unlikely to occur in unstructured situations (e.g.,Ware *et al.*, 1992). Consequently pupils with SLD may become isolated. In the USA, Gottman *et al.* (1975) and Luftig (1988), amongst others, have shown that 'retarded' students reported significantly more loneliness and isolation then did their mainstream peers in integrated settings. Other studies (e.g., Conway, 1988) have shown that pupils with SLD spend high percentages of time in isolation whilst being 'integrated' at play times. Such findings have important implications for pupils with SLD in integrated settings. Gottman *et al.* (1975) state that pupils with SLD may be subject to social isolation; but why are students with SLD so vulnerable in social settings? Research suggests that students with SLD have poorly developed social skills which may hinder integration (Gresham, 1981). This may, in turn, cause social rejection by mainstream peers (Strain, 1981).

Strain suggests a social behaviour intervention strategy which aids integration. It is a peer-mediated strategy which states that the peer mediating the treatment/intervention can be any child, not necessarily one who is developing normally. The peer social initiation can be used successfully with children exhibiting a more limited behaviour repertoire than the modelling approaches. This strategy could be developed within the foster friend/buddy system which operates within many integration schemes in the UK. However, one problem with such schemes is that the student with SEN may become an object of control, rather than an agent of control (this would equate with stage 3 – accommodation) hence never achieving equal status. In practical terms, mainstream peers may feel that they should 'look after' their friend. However, such friendships can be developed more positively on the lines of equal status, which benefits integration. Voeltz (1982), who used films, discussion sessions and direct contact with 'handicapped' students, noted that positive attitudes increased as a result of such an intervention

Equal status for pupils with SLD in mainstream settings may be structured in a variety of ways. Aronson and Bridgeman (1979) refer to Cohen's expectation theory (1972), which states that majority groups' competence results in dominance and superior achievement. Cohen suggests that alternatives be created to reverse these, often unconscious, expectations, and suggests a temporary exchange of majority and minority roles as a necessary prelude to equal status. Custer and Osguthorpe (1983) developed this concept in their research by teaching 'handicapped' students to instruct their non-handicapped peers in sign language. This was part of a study comparing social acceptance of handicapped students in mainstream schools. The same approach could be taught to other pupils with SLD in mainstream schools.

The contact hypothesis also affects academic classroom learning. In the classroom the teacher can structure activities and teaching to promote assimilation (functional integration) by selecting appropriate teaching methods to achieve goals. Deutsch (1949) conceptualized three types of goal structure in learning, which may be cross-referenced to stages in the contact hypothesis:

Deutsch (goal structure)		The contact hypothesis
1. Individualistic learning	results in	Sheer contact
2. Competitive learning	results in	Competition
3. Cooperative learning	results in	Accommodation/ Assimilation

There is a large body of research which suggests that cooperative teaching/learning methods are beneficial to integration. Johnson *et al.* (1983) suggest the jigsaw technique as a means of delivering cooperative teaching strategies to students in integrated settings. This method encourages all students to assume equal status and to work interdependently in pursuit of a common goal. It has proved successful if it is used for as little as 20 per cent of a child's time in class. An important note is that interdependent learning can co-exist easily with almost any other teaching method, alongside individualistic and competitive learning.

It is often the case that in individual learning situations, i.e. individual educational programmes, there is no correlation between the goal attainments of the participants. Whether an individual accomplishes his or her goal has no influence on whether other individuals achieve their goals. Consequently, a person seeks an outcome that is personally beneficial, ignoring as irrelevant the goal achievement efforts of other participants in the situation. This teaching method on its own is not conducive to integration as students would not reach beyond sheer contact stage.

A competitive teaching situation is one where Deutsch (op. cit,) notes that the goals of the separate participants are so linked that there is a negative correlation between the goal attainments. An individual can only attain his or her goal if other participants cannot attain their goals. This type of teaching on its own is not conducive to integration.

Returning to the original discussion, the notion that imitation of models occurs spontaneously is a myth. Gresham (1981) notes that many proponents of mainstreaming assume that placement of 'handicapped' children results in their emulating the appropriate academic and social behaviours of their peers. He notes that the assumption is a misconception of social learning theory, as modelling only occurs under certain conditions. Such observational learning is governed by four component processes: attention, retention, motor production and instruction. For modelling to occur the target subjects (pupils with SLD) are required to:

- attend to relevant modelling stimuli (perceive and attend to relevant components of the stimulus);
- retain information/stimuli (remember it);
- have motoric production processes necessary to perform the modelled behaviour (physical abilities);
- have an incentive or motivation for performing the observed behaviour (reinforcement).

From a theoretical perspective, successful integration of pupils with SLD into mainstream schools means actively meeting a number of conditions, rather than merely exposing the pupils to mainstream pupils and their teachers. This requires planning and intervention and consideration of the way the classroom is managed, and the way integration links are formed/arranged. Integration is a complex issue, and both the contact hypothesis and social learning theory share the assumption that the classroom environment will have to be modified for positive effects of integration to occur and that recreation times, i.e. play times, also need to be monitored so that friendships are nurtured and social isolation is avoided for pupils with SLD.

Conclusion

This chapter acknowledges that the first step in the integration process is being attempted across England and Wales. This is demonstrated by the number of initiatives which are being recorded, often in terms of statistics and case studies. However, such recordings lack evidence as to whether integration has been 'achieved' and there would appear to be no agreed criteria to measure its success.

The concept of integration needs to be readdressed. It is a complex issue which, until clearly defined in educational terms, is open to misinterpretation. Indeed, since it was formally introduced by Warnock (DES, 1978) and subsumed in the 1981 Education Act, this concept has continued to elude us. It is surely no wonder we have never attained it.

Integration cannot be measured solely by placement of pupils with learning difficulties in mainstream schools, or by academic achievement, social interaction, curriculum accessibility, human resources or physical resources. Although each of these elements is crucial to its success, it must be remembered that integration operates within a context. In this instance, the historical and current context is beset with negative attitudes and prejudices towards people with learning difficulties. Any integration initiative, therefore, must be aware of and sensitive to such attitudes which appear in many guises, often in easy attractive forms, under 'new' titles. Beware of such 'newnesses' and bandwagons in the integration revolution.

For integration to succeed, it is crucial that its objectives are defined and understood. To judge success they must be measured and evaluated. It is time to go beyond the current practice of 'tokenism'. In this country, more rigorous research urgently needs to be initiated where the outcomes of various integration programmes can be critically evaluated. This needs to go further than the current, limited, studies which show that certain settings and conditions can help or hinder the integration process. This would allow comparisons to be made with the more abundant literature from the USA.

What is needed is, perhaps, a scale of criteria which may be used to guide practice, progression and evaluation in relation to integration as a process. We need to be looking beyond placement and towards teaching and learning, contexts and conditions which will facilitate and enrich integration as a process.

References

Allport, G. (1954), *The Nature of Prejudice*, Reading, Mass: Addison Wesley.

Aronson, E. and Bridgeman, D. (1979), 'Jigsaw groups and desegregated classroom: in persuit of common goals, *Personality and Social Psychology Bulletin*, 5, 438–66.

Austin, M. and Gathercole, C. (1989), *Overdale: Integrating children with severe learning difficulties into mainstream schools*, Blackburn: North West Mental Handicap Development Team.

Bailey, J. F. (1988), 'Physically disabled pupils in mainstream schools', *Children and Society*, 2,2, 117–26.

Bandura, A. (1977) *Social Learning Theory*, Englewood Cliffs NJ: Prentice Hall.

Carpenter, B., Moore, J. and Lindoe, S. (1991) 'Changing attitudes', in Tilestone, C. (ed.) *Teaching Pupils with Severe Learning Difficulties*, London: David Fulton.

Cohen, E. (1972) 'Inter-racial, interaction, disability', *Human Relations*, 25, 1, 9–24.

Conway P. (1988) 'A Links System: An investigation and analysis of links between a school for pupils with severe learning difficulties and an ordinary school,' dissertation submitted in part fulfilment of the requirements leading to award of B.Ed. (Hons) Special Educational Needs, Special Educational Needs Centre. Didsbury School of Education.

Custer, J. D. and Osguthorpe, R. T. (1983) 'Improving social acceptance by training handicapped students to tutor their non handicapped peers', *Exceptional Children*, 50, 173–4

DES (1978) *Special Educational Needs* (The Warnock Report), London: HMSO.

DES (1981) *Education Act 1981*, London: HMSO.

DES (1993) *Education Act 1993*, London: HMSO.

Deutsch, M. (1949) 'An experimental sudy of the effects of co-operation and completion upon group process', *Human Relations* 2, 199–232.

Evans, P., and Ware, J. (1987) *Special Care Provision: The education of children with profound and multiple learning difficulties*, Slough: NFER-Nelson.

Gibb, C. and Donkersloot, P. (1991) 'Planning desegregation', *British Journal of Special Education*, 18,1, 33–5.

Gottman, J., Gonson, J. and Rasmussen, B. (1975) 'Social interaction, social competence and friendship in children', *Child Development*, 46, 700–18.

Gresham, F. M. (1981) 'Social skills training with handicapped children', *Review of Educational Research*, 139–76.

Howarth, S. B. (1987) *Effective Integration: Physically handicapped children in primary schools*, Slough: NFER-Nelson.

Humphreys, K. (1994) 'An irrational curriculum', *The SLD Experience*, Issue 9.

Jacklin, A. and Lacey, J. (1991) 'Assessing integration at Patcham House', *British Journal of Special Education*, 18, 2, 67–71.

Johnson, D.W., Johnson, R.T. and Maryuma, G. (1983) 'Interdependence and Inter-personal attraction among heterogeneous and homogeneous Individuals: A theoretical formulation and a meta-analysis of the research', *Review of Educational Research*, 53, 5–54.

Lalkhen, Y. and Norwich, B. (1990) 'The self-concept and self-esteem of adolescents with physical impairments in integrated and special school settings', *European Journal of Special Needs Education*, 5, 1, 1–11.

Lonton, T. and Farooqui, A. (1991) 'A disability curriculum for some', *British Journal of Special Education*, 18, 1, 29–31.

Luftig, R. (1988) 'Assessment of the perceived school loneliness and isolation of mentally retarded and non-retarded students', *American Journal on Mental Retardation*, 92, 5, 472–5.

Martlew, M. and Hodson, J. (1991) 'Children with mild learning difficulties in an integrated and in a special school: comparisons of behaviour, teasing and teachers attitudes', *British Journal of Educational Psychology*, 61, 355–72.

Ouvry, C. (1986) 'Integrating pupils with profound and multiple handicaps', *Mental Handicap*, 14, 157–60.

Samson, A. and Reason, R. (1988) 'What is successful re-integration? *British Journal of Special Education*, 15, 1, 19–23.

Sheldon, D. (1991) 'How was it for you? Pupils', parents' and teachers' perspectives on integration', *British Journal of Special Education*, 18, 3, 107–110.

Smith, G. and Goldthorpe, R. (1988) 'Returning to mainstream', *British Journal of Special Education*, 15, 4, 143–5.

Stobart, G. (1986) 'Is integrating the handicapped psychologically defensible?', *Bulletin of the British Psychological Society*, 39, 1–3.

Strain, P. (1981) 'Peer mediated teatment of exceptional children's social withdrawal', *Remedial and Special Education*, 1, 93–105.

Stukat, K. (1993) 'Integration of physically disabled students', *European Journal of Special Needs Education*, 8, 3, 249–68.

Tilstone, C., (ed.) (1991) *Teaching Pupils with Severe Learning Difficulties: Practical Approaches*, London: David Fulton.

Toon, C. (1988) 'Integrating children with severe learning difficulties into mainstream schools', *Education in the North*, 24, 42–52.

Voeltz, L. (1982) 'Effects of structured interactions with severely handicapped peers on children's attitudes', *American Journal of Mental Deficiency*, 86, 4, 153–8.

Ware, J., Sharman, M., O'Connor, S. and Anderson, M. (1992) 'Interactions between pupils with severe learning difficulties and their mainstream peers', *British Journal of Special Education*, 19, 4.

Williams, P. (1993) 'Integration of students with moderate learning difficulties. *European Journal of Special Needs Education*, 8, 3, 303–19.

CHAPTER 9

Discussion: Integration – Where do We Go From Here?

Peter Farrell

Introduction

The two preceding chapters illustrate the complex issues surrounding the arguments about the integration of children with SLD. They form an important contribution to the debate which, according to Hegarty (1993), has been at the heart of discussions about special education policy and practice for the past 25 years. Both chapters are challenging in their different ways. Hall confronts some of the unconscious assumptions which have been (and still are) prevalent in theory and practice in special education for many years and which have led to the development of special education services as they are today. He suggests that these assumptions have contributed to all children with SEN, including those with SLD, being offered an inferior education which consigns them to the devalued margins of society for the rest of their lives. His chapter leaves one feeling uncomfortable, as if those of us who have been wholly committed to helping children and their families with disabilities, have in fact achieved the opposite by allowing our unconscious assumptions to lead us to develop, maintain and support segregated provision.

Conway and Baker's chapter is also challenging as it draws from theory and research to illustrate just how difficult it actually is to achieve genuine social integration when children with disabilities are placed in integrated settings. It is simply not sufficient to arrange placements without giving a great deal of thought as to how the children will experience the social integration and inclusion which is being sought. Their chapter suggests that we are still some way from understanding how best we can achieve this goal.

This chapter considers the following key issues pertinent to the debate about the integration of children with SLD and, as each issue is discussed, reference will be made to the arguments raised in the previous two chapters:

- how might children with SLD experience integration?
- definitions of integration and inclusion;
- the arguments for and against the integration of children with SLD;
- research on integration;
- future provision for children with SLD.

How Might Children with SLD Experience Integration?

In recent years the term 'integration' has been used to describe a wide variety of educational provision which goes far beyond the three types outlined in the Warnock Report – namely locational, social and functional. Hegarty (1991) indicates that this could range from occasional visits by a child with a disability to a mainstream school, to full-time placement in such schools. It is therefore important, when discussing the potential benefits of integrated provision, to be absolutely clear about the type of integration which is under discussion. In this section a number of examples of different types of provision for children with SLD are discussed, each of which brings these children into contact with a more able peer group and could therefore be described as 'integrated'.

Full-time placement in a local neighbourhood school

This is equivalent to functional integration as originally described in the Warnock Report and is the only form of integration which is advocated by Hall. Children with SLD attend their local mainstream school, in a same-age class group throughout their school life, with support services being brought into the school. This would apply to all children with SLD no matter how severe their disability.

On the whole, functional integration as defined here is only offered to more able children with SLD, in particular children with Down's Syndrome, and there are many LEAs which are still reluctant to integrate any of their children with SLD, including those with Down's Syndrome. Integration, when it does occur, is likely to be for younger children, with only a few being integrated into secondary schools.

Full-time placement in a unit for children with SLD, housed within a mainstream school

This is equivalent to locational integration as described in the Warnock Report but, if the children spend all their time in the unit and never meet their mainstream peers, then the provision is little different from that of a special school. Nevertheless, there are a few examples which suggest that this unit model of integration has the potential to offer genuine opportunities for more inclusive provision. Perhaps the best known example is Bishopswood School in Oxfordshire (*TES*, 1992) where all the pupils, including those with PMLD, are placed in special classes in a primary and secondary school, both of which are close to the original special school. Bishopswood still exists as a separate school, although all its pupils are integrated in units within the mainstream primary or secondary school. A few LEAs, notably Stockport and Leeds, are developing similar schemes, and 'unit' models of integration have existed for many years in some rural areas, although there is little evidence of a wholesale move towards this type of integration across the country.

The placement of a whole class of children from an SLD school within a mainstream school

In this 'model' of integration, an SLD school links with a local mainstream school and arranges for one of its classes to transfer to the school. Indeed this was how the integrated provision at Bishopswood began. There are a few isolated examples where this type of provision has been arranged (for instance, Melland School, Manchester) although it is too early to say whether it will lead to more radical developments along the lines of Bishopswood.

Full-time placement of students with SLD in a unit based in a college of further education

Increasingly, colleges of further education are offering courses to more-able SLD students when they leave school. These students are usually taught in a separate room but they can be given opportunities to integrate with students in the rest of the college particularly for leisure activities and meal times.

Integrated nursery in an SLD school

In this model of integration, an SLD school opens its nursery to children from the local community who do not have learning difficulties, sometimes referred to as 'playgroup' children. Typically these nursery classes contain about 18 children, around half of whom have severe learning difficulties. When the playgroup children reach school age, they go to their local mainstream school. To label this provision as 'integrated' could be described as an exaggeration as there is a 50/50 balance between children with SLD and their more-able peers and because the children with SLD are in a special school.

Regular visits by pupils in an SLD school to a mainstream school

This is perhaps the most common way in which children with SLD experience opportunities to mix with their mainstream peers. However, here the children have no rights of access to the mainstream school. Arrangements are developed on a basis of goodwill. Over the past ten years there has been a growth in the number of SLD schools which have established informal links with local mainstream schools. This enables groups of children with SLD to visit mainstream schools on a regular basis, usually to join in a leisure activity. Jowett *et al.* (1988) found that well over 50 per cent of SLD schools had established such links. In a follow-up study, Fletcher-Campbell (1994) found that this number had increased to 70 per cent. The children are usually supported by staff from the special school who also arrange the transport; hence the arrangements are essentially informal and do not require the LEA to increase its expenditure. For some children these visits can be extended and may eventually lead to the full-time placement of a child in a mainstream school. Hall dismisses this type of integration as 'tokenistic', stating that its advocates do not have the 'slightest intention that it should develop into any worthwhile curricular or social integration' and that schools engage in it as a 'sop to their critics'. However, he quotes no evidence in support of his assertions.

Children with PMLD are 'integrated' into the classes of the SLD school

In all the literature on integration, the needs of children with PMLD tend to be overlooked. If a special school is seriously concerned about integrating its children into mainstream schools, then it hardly seems logical for it to maintain a separate special class within the SLD school for children with PMLD. However, many SLD schools do have such classes. It could be argued that an essential first step towards integration is to abandon PMLD classes and integrate the children within the remainder of the special school. Many schools are now organized in this way, although some have a adopted a flexible model, having a resource base for children with PMLD with regular opportunities for the pupils to join in activities with the rest of the school.

There are other ways in which children with SLD may come into contact with other children, for example visits from local mainstream children to a special school and the full- or part-time placement of children with SLD in another special school although, once again, these are only very 'mild' forms of integration. Indeed, this section has shown that children with severe learning difficulties can experience 'integration' in ways which are quite different from each other. Therefore, when discussing integration with parents and professional colleagues and when evaluating research findings, it is important to be clear about the level of integration being discussed.

The types of integration which have attracted the most publicity are full neighbourhood integration into a mainstream class and the unit model. However, the most common form of integration emanates from regular links between special and mainstream schools. Overall, it is important to remember that, despite initiatives towards integration which are taking place, the vast majority of children with SLD are still educated in special schools throughout their school life.

Definitions of Integration and Inclusion

In the previous section we have reviewed a variety of different types of provision, all of which might be described as 'integrated'. However, defining integration solely in terms of the provision a child receives tells us nothing about the quality of the education which is received in this provision. Are children placed in units attached to a mainstream school more 'integrated' than if they were taught in a special school? Jupp (1992a) argues that such units can be just as segregating. Similarly, a child with SEN placed in a mainstream class may in fact be isolated from the rest of the class and not truly 'integrated' within the group, particularly if he or she works with a support worker in one-to-one sessions for the majority of each day. Integrated placements, therefore, may still leave the child 'segregated'. When comparing the previous two chapters, it is interesting that although Conway and Baker discuss this problem in some depth, Hall makes no mention of it.

The term 'inclusion' has now become a more accepted way of describing the extent to which a child with SEN is truly 'integrated'. Indeed the pressure group which used to be known as the Centre for Studies on Integrated Education (CSIE) has now substituted 'Inclusive' for 'Integrated'. 'Inclusive education' and 'inclusion', therefore, are terms which are here to stay. Essentially, as Hall explains, they refer to the extent to which a school or community welcomes all people as a fully inclusive member of the group and values them for the contribution which they make. For integration to be effective the children must actively belong to, be welcomed by and participate in a mainstream school and community – that is, they should be fully *included*. Jordan and Powell (1994) provide a helpful discussion of the arguments about the meaning of the words 'integration' and 'inclusion'.

The challenge for parents and professionals is to ensure that, wherever possible, if children with SLD are educated in 'integrated' settings, they are also fully 'included'. This is a major challenge. Given the range and extent of their learning difficulties, in particular children with profound and multiple learning difficulties, there are huge problems in providing education which is genuinely inclusive and which also takes account of their individual needs.

The Arguments For and Against the Integration of Children With SLD

The previous section leads us on to a discussion of some of the arguments for and against integration. Who is likely to benefit from integration: the children themselves, their parents, teachers in mainstream and special schools, other children, society or a combination of all of these? Are there arguments in favour of certain types of integrated provision? Is there a case for maintaining a large special school sector?

Socio-political perspectives

Lindsay (1989) refers to many of the arguments in favour of integration as being socio-political. These arguments view integration as essentially a matter of human rights. The Centre for Studies on Inclusive Education (CSIE, 1989) advocates this view forcibly in their Integration Charter:

> We see the ending of segregation in education as a human rights issue which belongs within equal opportunities policies. Segregation in education because of disability or learning difficulty is a contravention of human rights as is segregation because of race and gender. The difference is that while sexism and racism are widely recognised as discrimination ... discrimination on the grounds of disability or learning difficulty is not.

This view is essentially the one advocated by Hall in his chapter and other writers (see, for example, Booth and Potts, 1983; Jupp, 1992b; Whitaker, 1992) take a similar view. These authors tend to use strong language to describe special schools and the practices that take place within them. For example they state that their very existence perpetuates a form of educational apartheid; they are sometimes described as ghettos; children in special schools are devalued; they are second-class citizens who are discriminated against; they are denied the same opportunities that are offered to their peers in mainstream schools.

It can be seen that socio-political arguments about integration are often expressed in language which is challenging and emotive. Those who favour a more flexible approach to special school provision for children with SEN (see, for example, Ouvry, 1994; Segal, 1993) take issue with the socio-political arguments on a number of counts. One of these concerns the issue of whether special schools devalue children and deny them equal opportunities; another concerns the arguments about human rights. Each of these is explored in more detail below.

According to the CSIE, children in special schools are devalued and are denied the same opportunities as their mainstream peers. This is a provocative statement which requires some analysis. Any visitor to a special school is likely to find that the children seem to be happy, that they experience a rich and stimulating education and that their teachers are keen and enthusiastic and enjoy teaching them. The children are offered a range of opportunities which are often far more extensive and challenging than they might experience in a mainstream school. How can such children be described as devalued? Do they feel devalued? Do their teachers, peers and parents devalue them? It could be argued that they would feel far more devalued and isolated in a mainstream class surrounded by unsympathetic teachers and children. To say that children in special schools are devalued and denied equal opportunities is at best simplistic and at worst wholly misleading.

The argument that placing children in special schools is a denial of basic human rights should also not go unchallenged. The United Nations has published a booklet on the rights of the child (United Nations, 1993). As regards children with disabilities, Article 23 states that, 'children should be helped to become as independent as possible and to be able to take a full and active part in everyday life'. Nowhere does it mention that these children should be taught in mainstream educational settings and, indeed, the aims of the Article are quite compatible with the notion that children with special needs may receive excellent education in special schools. The International League of Societies for Persons with Mental Handicap (Inclusion International) has recently published the Delhi Declaration on the Rights and Needs of Persons with Mental Handicap and their Families (ILSMH, 1994) which also makes no mention of the need to educate children with SEN in integrated settings. The views of the CSIE and others, therefore, appear to be out of step with current thinking on human rights.

The logical extension of their position that placing children in special schools represents a denial of human rights is that such schools should all be abolished. Therefore integrated education would be offered to all children with SEN. Would this deny parents and children the *right* of self-determination in that they would be denied the right to choose a special school for their child? As Lewis (1993) has asked,

> which is the more fundamental right: does a right to self determination over–ride the right to integrated education if the outcome of these two sets of rights come into conflict? (p.8)

Ouvry (1994) and Segal (1993) are also concerned that parents and children should be given the *right* to choose the provision for their children.

The key point about Article 23 of the UN Convention on Human Rights is that societies should do all they can to help children with disabilities become as independent as possible so that they can take a full and active part in everyday life. It is possible that high quality integrated education may make this more likely for children with SLD, but this remains an open question and special schools would undoubtedly claim that they are also doing all they can to achieve this aim.

'Empirical' arguments in favour of integration

As the above discussion illustrates, socio-political arguments about integration are contentious. Lindsay (1989) considers that there are also empirical arguments in favour of integration, which, unlike socio-political arguments, can be tested against research evidence. Some of these are referred to below in relation to children with SLD.

Children with SLD model appropriate behaviour from their mainstream peers
In particular it is argued that, in integrated settings, children with SLD benefit from being in a more language-enriched environment among a peer group whose behaviour is likely to be age-appropriate.

In mainstream schools, children with SLD will have access to a broader curriculum and increased resources
Because of their size, special schools do not have the equipment and facilities typically found in mainstream schools and that, as a result, their curriculum is too narrow and their resources restricted.

Placing children with SLD in mainstream schools raises parents' and teachers' expectations
Special schools are also segregating for parents and teachers and this can result in their expectations of what their children can do being reduced.

Parents prefer integration
One of the key arguments of pressure groups such as the CSIE is that parents are keen for their children with SLD to be integrated and that they have felt unduly pressurized to comply with a special school placement when faced with an array of 'experts'.

Integration benefits mainstream children, their parents and teachers
Including children with SLD in mainstream schools helps mainstream children and adults learn about the problems faced by those with disabilities and their families, and this contributes to society becoming more caring and compassionate. If we segregate, it is argued, we forget about those who could be described as less fortunate; if we ever meet children with SLD, we are afraid, we feel helpless, embarrassed and possibly antagonistic.

Arguments in favour of segregation

Some of the arguments in favour of segregated provision for children with SLD are discussed below.

The learning difficulties experienced by children with SLD are so great that it is unrealistic for them to share the same curriculum as that of their mainstream colleagues
This argument in favour of segregation does not apply to children with visual, hearing or physical difficulties where, with the careful adaptation of teaching materials and with specialized equipment, it is possible for them to work at the same level as their peers. Children with SLD, however, are likely to need a curriculum which is differentiated to such an extent that it bears no resemblance to that of their peer group. If this is the case, one has to question the level of integration which actually takes place when a child is working on such completely different tasks. This problem become more acute for older children and for pupils with profound and multiple learning difficulties.

The degree of careful planning required to teach children with SLD effectively can only be done in special schools
Not only do children with SLD require a highly differentiated curriculum, but a great deal of care and thought has to be given to how to teach it. This will be done more effectively by trained and experienced staff who are less likely to be available if children are integrated in mainstream schools throughout the LEA.

126

Specialist resources can be concentrated in one place
This includes the provision of speech and physiotherapy services, and facilities such as adapted toilets and multi-sensory rooms.

Teachers choose to teach children with SLD
The vast majority of teachers in SLD schools choose to work in such settings and find their work rewarding and intellectually challenging. In contrast, teachers in mainstream schools, who have an SLD child in their class, may not have any choice about the placement. They may be completely ignorant about the needs of such children and have no desire to teach them. They may also feel uncomfortable working alongside a support worker. This understandable reluctance may well affect the success of the integration.

It is easier to establish parent support groups in segregated settings
It is well known that parents of SLD children often value meeting other parents of similar children in order to share experiences and concerns. It is easier to establish parent groups if the children all go to the same school.

Children are in a peer group which is likely to be the same age and ability
A child with SLD in a mainstream class will almost certainly be the least able member of the group. This may affect his or her self-esteem and self-confidence. In a special school, he or she will be with peers of a similar ability and, as a result, it is easier to interact in a way which is enjoyable and meaningful, even though this may not be age-appropriate. It is difficult for children with SLD to engage in reciprocal play at a level which is genuinely interactive if their peer group consists of children who are much more able than they are.

It is safer in special schools
Special schools are smaller and better staffed than mainstream schools and therefore children with SLD, many of whom may have additional physical and sensory problems, are less likely to be at risk from large numbers of unruly children in a mainstream setting than they are in a special school.

It is more economical to teach children with SLD in special schools
Debates about integration often come down to this crucial point. According to the HMI/Audit Commission report (1992), it costs about £7,500 to educate a child with SLD in a day special school. It is often argued that, to be successfully integrated in a mainstream class, a child

with SLD requires the services of a support worker, possibly full time, and back-up support from an experienced teacher of children with SLD who visits on a weekly basis. This level of support costs the LEA more than it does to educate a child in an SLD school. However, if all special schools were to close down, then LEAs would make a saving and, as a result, the arguments about cost become more finely balanced.

Summary of the arguments for and against the integration of children with SLD

The socio-political arguments in favour of integration tend to be laced with emotive rhetoric about human rights. They can give the impression that, by definition, segregation is always bad and, as a result, the real achievements which have been made in special schools are not acknowledged. Empirical arguments in favour of integration suggest that there may be real social, linguistic and behavioural benefits from integration and that children and teachers in mainstream schools will also benefit. Arguments in favour of special schools focus on the problems of realistically meeting the curricular and social needs of children with SLD in a mainstream school and on the problems of allocating sufficient resources to the mainstream context.

Research on Integration

There is insufficient space in this chapter to provide a wide-ranging review of recent research on the integration of children with SLD. Extensive reviews of methodological issues and the research evidence are available elsewhere (see, for example, Danby and Cullen, 1988; Farrell, in press; Hegarty, 1993; Jenkinson, 1993; Lewis, 1995; Madden and Slavin, 1983; Zigler et al., 1990). The following observations are intended to summarize the main conclusions from recent research in this area.

- The complex methodological issues involved and the variability in the quality of the research which has been conducted makes it extremely difficult to compare the results of one study with another. In addition, many studies focus on the integration of children with a range of disabilities and, even if they focus on children with learning difficulties, it is not always easy to ascertain if they are referring to those who, in the UK, would be described as having SLD. In addition, the range of integrated provision being evaluated varies from study to study, resulting in further problems in making comparisons between them. These methodological problems are also referred to by Hall in his chapter.

- Notwithstanding these methodological concerns, the vast majority of studies report that children in mainstream schools accept their peers with disabilities and do not chastise or reject them.
- For integration to be successful it is vital for teachers, managers, local authority personnel, parents and children to be wholly committed.
- Mainstream and advisory teachers require training and support.
- Integration is more common and successful for younger children.
- Children with SLD in any setting require structured, carefully planned and differentiated teaching programmes.
- The degree of social and linguistic interaction between children with SLD and their peers is limited and tends to be didactic in nature. This is reinforced by Conway and Baker's analysis of the problems in fostering meaningful social interaction in mainstream classes between children with SLD and their mainstream peers.
- The attitudes of teachers in mainstream schools, in particular those who do not have a child with SLD in their class, are by no means uniformly positive. The more handicapped the child, the more negative the attitudes appear to be.
- Finally, the role of support staff is both complex and crucial. That children with SLD should be supported adequately by appropriately trained staff is not in question. However, research suggests that if support workers devote their time to the delivery of a carefully planned individual programme which undoubtedly helps the children to learn basic skills, opportunities for social interaction with their peer group become reduced. Moreover, the very act of teaching a child with SLD individually in a corner of the mainstream class may be viewed as segregation by all those involved, including the children. However, if the support worker devotes time to fostering social interaction, this may leave less time for individual teaching. Furthermore, it is by no means an easy task to foster social interaction between the children. If the child with SLD is simply placed with a group of mainstream children, he or she may be ignored; if the support worker joins in, this can influence the 'naturalness' of the interaction.

Future Provision for Children with SLD

So far in this chapter we have reviewed the arguments and the research about the integration of children with SLD and have related these to points made in the two previous chapters. What are the implications from this discussion for the future educational provision for these children? Have we reached the stage where there is sufficient evidence from research and a substantial commitment from parents and professionals to indicate that large-scale changes in provision for children with SLD should now be implemented? Is it sensible to continue to proceed towards increased integration through locally developed initiatives which exist at present? If these initiatives continue to develop and expand, the long-term existence of special schools will be called into question. Indeed, is there a future for special schools anyway? Is it possible to conceive of a model of educational provision for children with SLD which is integrated and inclusive, where children's needs are met, and which is adequately resourced?

In the remainder of this chapter we will consider three contrasting options for the long-term future of educational provision for children with SLD. These options are: neighbourhood integration, special schools with outreach, and special units in mainstream schools.

Option 1: Neighbourhood integration

This option would clearly be favoured by Hall. All children, regardless of their disability, would go to their local school where additional support and resources would be provided. Such placements already exist for a number of primary-age children with SLD, but they are extremely rare in secondary schools.

Although there are many arguments in favour of this type of provision, which are explored earlier in this chapter, and some evidence that younger children at the top end of the SLD range may benefit, there are a number of concerns which suggest that it may not be suitable for the majority of children with SLD. First, as children get older, the gap in attainments and curricular needs between those with SLD and their mainstream peers becomes increasingly large. This means that the curriculum has to be even more differentiated, to the extent that the children are rarely doing similar work. This may inevitably result in children with SLD being segregated within the mainstream school. Second, the difficulties in fostering social interaction are more acute for older and more disabled children. Third, there is some evidence (Blacher and Turnbull, 1982) that parents of children with SLD can feel isolated if their child attends the local school, as they have less in common with other parents with whom it is difficult to share the experience of bringing up a child with a disability. Fourth, it is difficult to see how children with PMLD would benefit from neighbourhood integration as their curricular needs are so different from their peer group. If children with PMLD are excluded from neighbourhood integration, where should they be educated? Is it educationally sensible for them to remain as a separate group in a special school containing, for example, children with physical disabilities?

For some children, however, neighbourhood integration may be an effective option, particularly if it is started at an early age, and for children who are at the top end of the SLD range. However, as an option for all children with SLD, including those with PMLD, it is probably not viable.

Option 2: Special schools with outreach

This is the most common form of integration, as Jowett *et al.* (1988) and Fletcher-Campbell (1994) have indicated. Virtually all special schools for children with SLD have developed contacts with local mainstream schools which enable many of their children to experience opportunities to interact with their mainstream peers. Indeed, some special schools have appointed additional staff to fulfil this role. This is, however, the least radical form of integration, and indeed to call it 'integration' could be described as grossly exaggerated. There are obvious advantages for special schools as their continued existence, far from being threatened, is guaranteed or even enhanced to that of a resource centre which has the potential to offer support and advice across the mainstream sector.

There are, however. major logistical problems for SLD schools to overcome in managing this form of integration. For example transport has to be organized and coordinated; it may take time to establish links and to provide the necessary support and training for mainstream staff; and there needs to be adequate staff cover for the children who are left behind in the special school and for the integrated children. Furthermore, if some children are placed in mainstream schools for considerable periods of time each week, for example up to three days, then one has to question whether such a 'part-time' option may leave them with a sense of not belonging to either establishment. However, unless schools provide opportunities for this form of integration to become more substantial, it will remain nothing more than tokenistic.

Option 3: Special units in mainstream schools

In two earlier articles (Farrell and Sugden, 1985; Mittler and Farrell, 1987), a unit model of integrating children with severe learning difficulties was proposed as providing the best opportunity for these children to experience the full benefits of integration while at the same time ensuring that their educational needs are met. This model is summarized in Table 9.1.

Table 1: Unit model of integration in mainstream schools
(Take from Mittler and Farrell, 1987)

School	Pupils	Units	Teachers	Assts
Primary	20	2	3	4
Primary	20	2	3	4
Secondary	30	3	4	6
FE College	10	1	1.5 +2 Sen Ts 1 Dep HT 1 HT	1
Total	80	8	15.5	15

It is important to point out that the unit model of integration is not a new idea and already exists in some parts of the country; Bishopswood School being the best known example (*TES*, 1992). There are a few other examples of similar initiatives being developed (for example, in Stockport) but overall progress has been slow, although similar arrangements operate in other countries (Forlin, in press).

Under this unit model it is assumed that the whole population of a school for children with SLD, including those with PMLD, would be relocated into two primary schools, one secondary school and one further education college. There would be a total of eight units, with a notional ten children per unit, with two units in each of the primary schools, three in the secondary school and one in the FE college. Although the model represented in Table 9.1 assumes that there would be a total of 80 children, it could easily be adapted in line with the basic principles being outlined, whatever the numbers. The model could also apply, with some modifications, if children with a broader range of SEN, including moderate learning and physical difficulties, were included in the units.

It would be important for each of these settings – the primary and secondary schools and the FE college – to be carefully selected to ensure that all staff were committed to the integration of children with SLD, and that there were appropriate classrooms within the buildings. It would not be appropriate for these units to be placed in a separate classroom block on the other side of the playground.

The staffing ratios in this model are more generous than those currently available in special schools. This is justified in terms of the additional support work needed in mainstream classes to support integrated children. The closure of special schools would also provide considerable savings in capital maintenance and overheads which could be used to support these additional staffing levels.

The headteacher, who would carry overall responsibility for the education of all 80 children, would probably be based in the secondary school. He or she would have responsibilities for coordination and communication across the eight units with the headteachers and staff in the host schools, and would also carry responsibility for liaison with the LEA and other relevant agencies. Clearly, headteachers would have an unusual and demanding role. They would need to coordinate scattered and dispersed staff and services, while providing firm leadership and personal and professional support. They would also have responsibility, together with the deputy headteacher, for planning and coordinating staff training both for their own special needs staff in the mainstream school and the FE college.

The amount and nature of integration experienced by each of the children would depend on their agreed and assessed needs. Integration would vary along a continuum. For example, children with PMLD might only experience locational and some social integration. For children at the other end of the continuum, full-scale functional integration might be possible for increasing periods of time. Each child's need for appropriate locational, social and functional integration would be continuously reviewed.

The establishment of a scheme of this nature would not preclude the neighbourhood integration of some children whose parents request it. Staff supporting such children could be attached to the staff of the schools outlined in this model in order to avoid professional isolation.

Conclusion

In my view, the unit model of integration, outlined above, is the one which can form the basis for a flexible range of inclusive education which will meet the individual needs of all children with SLD. It is the one which is most compatible with Article 23 of the United Nations statement on the rights of the child, referred to earlier in this chapter. The model is clearly a compromise between the more extreme neighbourhood integration model and the 'special schools with outreach' approach. But it is also progressive in that it allows for tailor-made inclusive education programmes to be implemented for the full range of children with SLD, which could include neighbourhood education in some cases. The model is radical as its implementation would result in the closure of special schools as they exist at present and it is therefore unlikely that it will take place overnight. Instead it is possible that, within the next ten years, there will be a gradual but steady increase in the number of carefully planned, resourced and evaluated unit-based models of integration, so that this model of provision will eventually be the norm.

Note
This contribution has been adapted from two chapters which will appear in Farrell, P. (in press) *The Education of Children with Severe Learning Difficulties*, London: Cassell.

References

Blacher, J. and Turnbull, A. (1982) 'Teacher and parent perspectives on selected social aspects of preschool mainstreaming', *The Exceptional Child*, 29, 3, 191–9.

Booth, T. and Potts, P. (1983) *Integrating Special Education*, Oxford: Blackwell.

CSIE (1989) *The Integration Charter*, London: Centre for Studies on Inclusive Education.

Danby, J. and Cullen, C. (1988) 'Integration and mainstreaming: a review of the efficacy of mainstreaming and integration for mentally handicapped pupils', *Educational Psychology*, 8, 3, 177–95.

Farrell, P and Sugden, M. (1985) 'Integrating children with severe learning difficulties: fantasy or reality?', *Education and Child Psychology*, 8, 69–80.

Farrell, P. (in press) *The Education of Children with Severe Learning Difficulties*, London: Cassell.

Fletcher-Campbell, F. (1994) *Still Joining Forces?*, Slough: NFER.

Forlin (in press) 'Educators' beliefs about inclusive practices in Western Australia', To appear in the *British Journal of Special Education*.

HMI/Audit Commission (1992) *Getting in on the Act*, London: HMSO.

Hegarty, S. (1991) 'Towards an agenda for research in special education', *European Journal of Special Needs Education*, 6, 2, 87–99.

Hegarty, S. (1993) 'Reviewing the literature on integration', *European Journal of Special Needs Education*, 8, 3, 194–200.

ILSMH (1994) *The Delhi Declaration on the Rights and Needs of Persons with Mental Handicap and their Families*, Brussels: ILSMH.

Jenkinson, J. C. (1993) 'Integration of students with severe and multiple learning difficulties', *European Journal of Special Needs Education*, 8, 3, 320–35.

Jordan, R. and Powell, S. (1994) 'Whose curriculum? Critical notes on integration and entitlement', *European Journal of Special Needs Education*, 9, 1, 27–39.

Jowett, S., Hegarty, S. and Moses, D. (1988) *Joining Forces*, Slough: NFER.

Jupp, K. (1992a) 'What are we waiting for?', *Learning Together*, 2, 9–10.

Jupp, K. (1992b) *Everyone Belongs*, London: Souvenir Pres.

Lewis, A. (1993) *Integration in Practice: Learning difficulties*, University of Birmingham, School of Education, Distance Learning Material.

Lewis, A. (1995) *Children's Understanding of Disability*, London: Routledge.

Lindsay, G. (1989) 'Evaluating integration', *Educational Psychology in Practice*, 5, 1, 134–43.

Madden, N. A. and Slavin, R. F. (1983) 'Mainstreaming students with mild handicaps: academic and social outcomes', *Review of Educational Research*,

134

53, 4, 519–89.

Mittler, P. and Farrell, P. (1987) 'Can children with severe learning difficulties be educated in ordinary schools?', *European Journal of Special Needs Education*, 2, 221–36.

Ouvry, C. (1994) 'The great integration debate: part 4', *British Journal of Learning Disabilities*, 22, 1, 27–30.

Segal, S. (1993) 'The great integration debate: Part 2', *Mental Handicap*, 21, 109–111.

Times Educational Supplement (1992) 'Secure in a special school without its own front door', 1 May.

United Nations (1993) *The Rights of the Child*, New York: Department of Health, Children's Rights Development Unit.

Whitaker, J. (1992) 'Can anyone help me to understand the logic of Snoezelen?', *Learning Together*, 2, 23–4.

Zigler, E., Hodapp, R. M. and Edison, M. R. (1990) 'From theory to practice in the care and education of mentally retarded individuals', *American Journal of Mental Retardation*, 95, 1, 1–12.

Index

LEAs (local education authorities), 108,
118, 119, 120, 125, 127, 132
Leeds, 16, 119
legislation, 15, 16, 85, 91, 92-3, 103 see
also names of Acts
lessons, sharing, 100
Lewis, A., 124, 127
Lindsay, G., 122, 124
link integration, 104, 106, 121
'Living your Life' (Craft and Members
of the Nottinghamshire SLD Sex
Education Project), 26
local education authorities see LEAs
local level, self-advocacy at, 6-7
locational integration, 99, 118
Lodge, Christopher, 9
Lodge, Mary, 9
London, 4
London Borough of Hounslow, 34
Lonton, T., 109
Lovett, Herb, 98
Luftig, R., 111

McCormick, L., 49
McGill University, 98
McKinlay, Ian
article by, 38-44
textual references to, 39, 44
Madden, N. A., 127
Mahoney, G., 77
mainstream schools, integration into
arguments in favour of, 124-5, 127
children's experience of, 86, 118-9,
120
desirability of, 98
and future provision, 129-33
and inclusion, 99, 122
and legislation, 103
practice of, 104, 106, 107, 108-9
research on, 128
theories about, 110-4
and units, 107, 118-9, 121, 130-2,
133
see also integration; primary schools;
secondary schools
Manchester, 119
marriage, 43
Martlew, M., 107
massage sessions, 35, 44

masturbation, 27-8, 30, 35, 42, 44
Matson, J.L, 58, 73
medical model of disability, 88-9, 92,
94
Melland School, 119
MENCAP, 5
menstruation, 21, 22, 38-9, 40, 41
Miller, R., 85
Mittler, Peter
article by, 1-13
textual references to, 12, 130, 131
MLD (moderate learning difficulties),
104, 107-8
modelling, 110, 113, 124
moderate learning difficulties (MLD),
104, 107-8
Montreal, 98
mother:child interactions, 77
motives, 33
motor production process, 113
Musselwhite, C., 67

National Children's Bureau, 93
National Curriculum, 10, 62-3, 83, 86,
105, 106, 108
national level, self-advocacy at, 4-6
national organizations, 4-5
needs, 92-3, 93-4, 95-8
negative feelings and attitudes, 33, 111,
114, 128
neighbourhood integration, 121, 129-
30, 132
Nichols, P., 33
Nind, Melanie
article by, 48-56
textual references to, 54, 55, 71, 73,
75
Nirje, B., 50, 74
Noonan, M.J., 49
normalization, 8, 15, 29, 49, 50, 51, 52,
53, 54, 71-2, 89-90
Norris, J.A., 51
North Americans, 50, 53, 99
Norwich, B., 109
Nottinghamshire SLD Sex Education
Project, 26
Nottingham University Department of
Learning Disabilities, 25
nursery, 119-20

140

O'Brien, John, 98
observational learning, 113
Oliver, M., 78
opinions, importance of, 13
Osguthorpe, R.T., 112
Ouvry, C., 104, 105, 123, 124
overprotection, 1
Oxfordshire, 119

paradigms
  definition of, 87-8
  inappropriate, 89, 94
  models within, 88-90
paraprofessionals, 73
parents
  and age-appropriateness, 19, 62, 74
  and bonding, 29
  and integration debate, 122, 124,
    125, 126, 128, 129
  interactions with child, 77
  and self-advocacy, 1, 2, 4, 5-6, 7, 8,
    9-11, 12, 13
  and sexuality, 16, 17, 18, 19, 22, 26,
    28, 31-4, 38-44
  see also family
Park, Keith
  article by, 58-68
  textual reference to, 70
Patten, John, 16
Patton, M.Q., 88
PD (physical disabilities), 104, 108-10
Pearpoint, Jack, 98
peers, 74, 100, 101, 106, 110, 111-2,
  120, 124, 125, 126, 128, 129, 130
periods see menstruation
personal autonomy see autonomy,
  personal
personal hygiene, 39, 41
person-appropriateness, 79
physical appearance, interest in, 41
physical disabilities (PD), 104, 108-10
Piaget, J., 51, 75
placement, 110, 111, 114, 117, 118,
  119, 121
playgroup children, 119
play times, 111, 114
PMLD see profound and multiple
  learning difficulties
policies, development of, 34-6

political correctness/incorrectness, 33,
  83, 85
Porter, Jill
  article by, 58-68
  textual references to, 70, 74, 75
Potts, P, 122
Powell, A., 77
Powell, S., 122
Power, T., 38
power relationships, 78
pregnancy, 42
Pre-School Playgroup Association, 20
primary prevention, 6
primary schools, 16, 106, 107, 119, 129,
  131
  see also mainstream schools; schools
Pringle, Mia Kellmer, 93
professionals
  and age-appropriateness, 73
  and case conferences, 7
  failure to get to know child, 98
  and families, 8, 9, 11, 12
  and human error, 85
  and integration, 83, 122, 128-9
  and needs, 92, 93, 94, 95
  and objectives, 78
  as obstacle to self advocacy, 5
  and PMLD pupils, 105
  and sex education, 16
  and sexuality, 17, 26
  and society, 101
  see also staff/teachers
profound and multiple impairment
  and self-advocacy, 9, 11
  and sexuality, 25-36
  see also profound and multiple
  learning difficulties
profound and multiple learning
  difficulties (PMLD), 104-6, 120,
  122, 125, 129, 130,
  131, 132 see also profound and
  multiple impairment
project groups, 26-7, 35, 36
provocative behaviour, 42
psychologists, 51, 84
puberty, onset of, 38-9
pupils
  and age-appropriateness, 61-2, 63-4,
  65-6
  integration of see integration

142

social acceptance, 73-4, 75, 78, 90
social and communication
    development, concentrating on see
    intensive interaction
social behaviour intervention strategy,
    111-2
social devaluation, 89-90, 91, 117, 123
social integration, 99, 105, 106, 109,
    111, 117, 118
social interaction, 41, 128, 129 see also
    interaction
social isolation, 111, 114
social justice, 99 see also human rights
social learning theory, 110, 113, 114
social life, 23
social model of disability, 89
social role valorization, 49, 50, 71, 89-
    90 see also normalization
social workers, 22
society, 49-50, 51, 52, 58, 71, 72, 78,
    101, 117, 125
    see also social acceptance; social
    devaluation
socio-political arguments for
    integration, 122-4, 127
spastic quadriparesis, 39
special educational needs (SEN) pupils,
    integration of see integration
special interest groups, 4-5
special needs education
    discussion of needs, 92-8
    models for, 86, 88-9
    and social value, 91
    see also integration; schools,
    segregation; special schools
special schools
    and age-appropriateness, 63-4
    arguments against, 101, 122-4
    arguments for, 125-7
    closure of, 131-2
    and future provision, 129, 130
    and integration, 15, 85-6, 104, 105,
    106-7, 108, 109, 119-21, 130
    and opportunities for choice and
    decision-making, 10
    and physically disabled pupils, 108-9
    practice in,92
    and sex education, 17
    and social value, 91
    unconscious assumptions about, 83-

5, 117
    see also integration; schools;
    segregation; special needs education
special units see units/unit model of
    integration
staff/teachers
    and age-appropriateness, 49, 61-2,
    65-6, 67, 68
    careful planning by, 125
    choice of work, 126
    and cognitive dissonance, 84
    and contact hypothesis, 112
    and expectations of children, 124
    and intensive interaction, 48
    and logistical problems, 130
    in mainstream schools, 106, 108,
    126, 128
    and PMLD pupils, 105
    role in laying foundations for self-
    advocacy, 2, 9-11, 77-8
    and service users' preferences, 79
    and sex education, 16, 17
    and sexuality, 17, 18, 20, 26, 28, 29,
    31-4, 35, 36, 38, 40
    and unit model of integration, 131,
    132
    see also professionals
sterilization, 43 see also hysterectomy
Stobart, G., 110
Stockport, 119, 131
Strain, P., 111-2
Structure of Scientific Revolution, The
    (Kuhn), 87
student committees, 6
Stukat, K., 109-10
Sugden, M., 130
support work, 2, 3, 108, 109, 118, 127,
    128, 131
Szivos, S.E., 52

teachers see staff/teachers
teenagers see young people
therapeutic curriculum, 92
therapeutic input, 104, 106
Thomson, J., 15
Tilstone, C., 106
toilet, 39
Toon, C., 104, 106
Toronto, 4
transport needs, 93